THINGS YOUR THERAPIST CAN'T SAY

Things Your Therapist ~~Can~~ <u>Can't</u> Say...

COUPLES' EDITION

BY JENNIFER M. BANKS
REGISTERED PSYCHOTHERAPIST

To my parents,

Thank you for showing me what a loving relationship looks like...

Table of Contents

Prologue

Picture it: Sicily, 1955. Well, not quite—but close. We were in Brampton, Ontario in 2004, and it was a scorcher of a day. Temperatures were at a record high and my husband Paul would make a decision that would impact the rest of his life. He had a horrible habit of drinking black coffee, smoking cigarettes, and not eating until dinner since eating would slow his work down. This day was no different than any other day, except his adrenaline was pumping faster than the sun was hitting the pavement. It was a day I will never forget and a look that is forever etched into my mind. I would do anything to be able to erase the image that has haunted me for almost twenty years...

Paul, dripping in sweat, working at perfecting his craft, screamed, "Ouch!"

"What happened?!?" I exclaimed.

"I can't believe it! I just shot myself with the nail gun!" he replied.

Paul, yanked out the nail he had shot into his left hand while putting up crown moulding in our future home. The minor annoyance didn't make Paul flinch, rather, the ruined piece of wood was his biggest concern. Paul didn't stop working and refused to miss a beat. Rather, he then did what he did best, which was continue to work without a break. His anger was palpable, as was his frustration. I hated being around his anger, I always felt so uncomfortable and helpless; something I have learned to manage throughout our years together.

As Paul stood there with his anger, I decided to give him some space and went to get something with which to bandage him. Upon my return, his demeanour hadn't changed. He started breathing a little heavier, and found his way outside to cool off from the annoyance. He lit a cigarette, was full of sweat, and then his face went to one deathly shade of gray. His cigarette was a mountain of ashes, ready to fall, as he took another drag. But in that moment, life as we knew it, forever changed.

Paul mumbled, "I don't feel so g–..." He fell. Hard. Tumbling forward, cigarette intact, singeing his unshaven skin.

I started to scream as I looked at his still body, face smashed into the concrete. It was like an episode of Criminal Minds; blood everywhere, and his missing parts beside him. Maybe a little dramatic– but there were missing teeth. (I lost myself there as if I were Baby Girl and Derek Morgan...) Ok, focus, *where was I?*

Paul lay there, still, as I screamed at the top of my lungs. I turned him over, peeled back the cigarette that had melted into his face, attempting to wake him up. He finally came back to me, still white as a ghost, full of blood, with a mouth vacated of teeth, and asked, "What happened? Where are my teeth?" Paul had passed out from heat exhaustion and excessive adrenaline. He was in shock and couldn't feel his legs. I ran and grabbed a phone to call 911.

All of a sudden, he said his legs were tingling and the feeling was coming back. He was able to sit up as I held his chin up to his face—where it had been just a few minutes before. I was in utter shock as I started collecting all the teeth scattered around the crime scene that were once a part of my beloved Paul's face. The smile that I noticed so many years back that brought me to notice him the first day we met; the smile that highlighted his cute dimples that made me weak in the knees, had completely vanished.

That was the first day of the rest of our lives… and it was going to break us before it made us.

I Know who I am, I'm not, & I'll never be

"Better to be a king for a night than a schmuck for a lifetime!"
—ROBERT DENIRO—

As a Registered Psychotherapist I have always strived to be able to spell it correctly, and to be able to relate to my clients through transparency, as a fellow human being. This may sound funny to you, but from my own experience receiving counselling, I have always benefited greatly from a session with a therapist who shows that they bleed red too. However, not all therapists are created equally.

I'll never forget the time a therapist told me I was "needy." I was a young twentysomething, newly-married and in trouble. My husband and I had both been attending individual and couple sessions with the same therapist. (Highly unethical, I *now* know! If you and your partner are seeing a therapist together, you should not have the same therapist for individual sessions.). We had just had our son, and I was in a deep, dark place with postpartum depression. The depression set in instantly after giving birth to our wonderful child. However, I had zero confidence as a new mother. I didn't know who I was anymore, and I was riddled with anxiety for the first time in my life. That anxiety became a part of me, and it persists to this day. She's a monster who won't leave me alone; but keeps me sitting in fear when I indulge her. A dual-headed monster who also keeps me safe from all that I fear. I have learned, consequently, to manage her well—most of the time.

Anxiety is a funny thing. We need a little bit of it, but not too much. We want it at specific times, but not in others. And, we want to choose when it comes out, not allow it to choose the timing—almost like a mother in law. Anxiety exists in all of us. It can keep us from running into traffic. Or it can keep us from going into a lion's den. It can also keep us totally immobilized, and stuck at home instead of going to that event where there would be a crowd of people.

The anxiety I had postpartum stopped me from enjoying moments with my newborn son. I was scared and worried most of the time, as a new mom who had no clue what she was doing. On top of that, I lived in the country, on a snow belt in northern Ontario, and it was during the winter of 2011 when we had record-breaking snow falls. To say I was stuck, is an understatement (and the literal truth). But I have always been the type of person who asks for help when I am stuck and feeling alone. This happened to be the most alone I had ever felt.

It takes effort and courage to seek help, mixed with a little hope. I was desperate for anyone to say, *it'll be alright*. My beautiful newborn baby needed me, and I longed for the confidence I saw in other mothers. I knew I couldn't go it alone, so I made a doctor's appointment as a first step. My doctor was fantastic, and was instrumental in helping me on my journey with postpartum depression. She told me to start some medication, start some counselling, and *stop being a one-track breastfeeding lunatic and give the baby a bottle.* This was the best advice I received up until that point since I wasn't producing enough milk anyway, but felt like I would be failing if I gave in to buying formula. She let me off the hook that day, a day in which I felt soaked with shame and embarrassment. She also started me on some anxiety meds, which was new territory for me. These two things alone made a huge impact on my ability to cope. The last piece of advice was to seek out a counsellor with whom to talk, which I readily did. I started seeing a counsellor who seemed nice, reasonably priced, and had availability. I was totally green and had never embarked on the hunt for a shrink. This was all new territory.

The counselling was helpful at first. I spilled my guts about feeling so alone and not knowing who I was anymore. She listened, validated, and suggested that Paul come in too so we could meet with her as a couple. Paul agreed. He had always been supportive, and had gone along with most things I presented to him. So we went together and started to talk about our relationship.

We had been married for 5 years and were still learning how to be married. I was fragile in that office, Paul was tired, and the counsellor asked me to describe how alone I felt. Just as I finished, Paul grew frustrated with me. He didn't know what I wanted and what else he could do. At this moment, the counsellor dropped a bomb on me that blew me into millions of tiny pieces that are still trying to reassemble themselves. Instead of validating me, a fragile new mother with a three week old baby, she psychoanalyzed me and called me the meanest name I had ever been called. A name that paralyzed me for years during emotional breakdowns and conflicts. A name that I have carried with me everywhere I go. She called me... *needy*.

I left the office in a worse state than that in which I'd gone in; a heaviness like a ton of bricks escorted me back home. The choice of words the counsellor used the day I was so desperately looking for support, filled me with shame and embarrassment, as if I had broken a commandment: "Thou shall not be *needy*..." One word. One single, two syllable word affected me like the plague—for years. Not only did it hurt; but from then on, I was labelled, in our marriage, as *the needy one*. Imagine, someone who is supposed to be a positive advocate decides to analyze you instead, and sends you home with a new complex—and a bill to pay! Sounds pretty crappy to me, and it was.

I remember thinking, *Well, excuse me. I didn't know our troubled marriage was all my fault and that wanting to have an emotional connection with my "newish" husband was out of the ordinary.* At the same time, I was unaware that the post vaginal pushing of a watermelon-sized human out of my loins and having every drop of the feel-good baby hormone seep out of me, was, well, needy. One word. I felt so small in the room, and had visions of the therapist towering over me at 10 feet tall, laughing with my husband in slow motion... "Y O U A R E S O O O O N E E D Y... HAHAHAHA...," repeating the sentence, as if ten voices were telling me at once, from every direction. The saddest part of this scene that I catastrophized in my mind was that... I believed it. Shame sunk in. Shame stayed with me like a bad smell. For years.

Not only did the feeling of *neediness* last for years; it wove its way into my history, causing me to assume that I'd been needy for ages. Here's how: The accident was a pivotal moment in our relationship. Paul underwent surgeries that were so major, he had restrictions that would become lifelong. His pride, as a man, was damaged as much as his spinal cord had been. As a result, my husband became distant in the first six months after the accident. This left me with the familiar pang of being alone. Feeling alone and longing to fix it, often leads us to seek out comfort, which can look like neediness. When you're alone, what you want and what you need is love.

We did, however, receive a ton of help from family and friends; people continually offered support. But one thing of which I'm cognizant, because of my experience as a caregiver, is to check-in on other caregivers. Paul had been the centre of attention, and rightly so. But I had gone through this *with* him, yet it had been a lonely experience. I don't ever remember being asked by anyone how I was coping. This isolated me further. Being alone can be scary and can instill fear. When I say "alone," I don't mean without others around. I mean an inner feeling of being alone, or a *void*. One in which no amount of people can fill. In the next chapter, we'll explore what that void may be and how to start appreciating being alone. Suffice to say, I felt alone and rewrote my history as "the needy wife" after our experience with counselling.

Paul and I did our best through those newlywed years, nevertheless. There were times in which he could work, and times when he couldn't; his body was so unpredictable. In spite of looking so able-bodied, he was anything but. We never knew from one day to the next what would happen with his body and nerves that were so badly damaged. Life was unpredictable; and that unpredictability prevented us from getting a good start on our marriage. So, we continued with the marriage counselling. We also did relationship weekends, where I leaned on other women in my life while Paul looked for support from other men. We worked hard to stay together. Divorce was never on the table; we were committed. Needy or not, we were going to figure this marriage out, together.

Through this process I learned that it turns out that having needs is "normal." This spawned the realization that, *damn right I was needy!* And I learned that there was no shame in that. Rather, the neediness stemmed from a void that was created by past trauma, a lack of affection, and many other situations in my life in which I sought attention in the wrong places.

As a child, I was alone very often. I was lonely, and often bored. Being lonely as a child was difficult. My parents ran a very successful business which demanded multiple hours of their time; which meant I was on my own for the better part of most days. My siblings were off to university and had each other. I was much younger than them, so I felt like an only child much of the time. As a result, I learned how to cook and take care of myself as a young teenager. I should mention that my folks always made sure I was taken care of, and loved me unconditionally. They were (and are) incredible parents, and continue to be. For Dutch immigrants, the key to their success was work, work, and then more work. Sundays were a day of rest, which included church and roast beef supper cooked the Dutch way—well done! My parents were workers who sacrificed to make the most wonderful life for their three children. And a wonderful life they did make. (Only I can't stand roast beef anymore.)

As an adult and therapist, I know that the void I was feeling wasn't fulfilled by the wonderful life they provided. I was lonely; not always alone, but lonely. What a huge difference this can be. You can be in a crowded room and feel alone, or be alone in a canoe in the middle of a lake and feel so fulfilled, supported, and at peace. Regrettably, the reality for so many children is loneliness; we can't buy love that has a true emotional connection. Lives filled with things, presents, activities, and the best opportunities will not fill the void of emotional connection.

THE STORY OF RACHEL...

Rachel was a student at one of the schools at which I worked as a school counsellor. She came from a home that had endless money, fancy cars, and everything that came with extreme wealth. Her mother would pick her up in her Jaguar SUV and would drop her off at the stables where she would tend to one of three horses she owned. Now, Rachel was a pretty smart girl who, on the outside, looked like she had it made. But on the inside, she was really struggling. She would share with me how much she wished her mother would be home, or how she yearned for her siblings to ask her to do something after school.

My mother is so caught up in her own life, she didn't even notice when I grabbed the bottle of wine from the fridge and walked past her. I did it to test her. I knew she wouldn't notice, I just knew it.

Did you tell her?

Yes, I walked to the table and slammed the bottle down and told her. She freaked on me! Can you believe it? That bitch took it out on me

instead of admitting she was too busy swiping left and swiping
right, just to get her thrills with some dude. I am so sick of it. My dad
would freak out if he was here. She's changed so much since he left.

Rachel was alone and lonely. It turns out that the wealthiest student I had worked with, was one of the most lonely kids I had encountered. It's interesting to note that the void Rachel was feeling could present as "neediness" (cringe) from the outside, when it was really her way of searching for a means to fill the void. Children ask for attention in some of the most seemingly illogical ways. Picking on others, vandalism, self harm such as cutting or risky behaviours (which is more prominent in boys), sexual encounters, drugs, alcohol, porn, and all the other problems we see today in our children, are all ways to fill a void. The void hurts and lingers, it pops up when teachers talk, parents yell, and when the bully at school is cruel. The void is the root cause, while the long list above are the symptoms. Rachel was a defiant teenager who struggled to make friends. Over the school year, her academic performance began to slip, which caused her mother to blame the school. Eventually, Rachel was sent to private school. It wouldn't end up being the solution that Rachel's mom hoped for. It marked the beginning of a sad end to an even sadder story—one of many sad stories amongst the throngs of children who are all trying to fill their voids with destructive tendencies.

One of the reasons I became a therapist was to help kids like Rachel. Today, I try to be the adult I needed when I was her age. Not a mom or dad, but a caring adult, outside of the family, to whom I could have spoken when I felt so alone. I had no one to talk to about my true loneliness, I was too ashamed. As a result, I was alone, in spite of the love that ran deeply through our family. The loneliness was, at times, so painful that I eventually figured out a way to distract myself from those feelings.

All it took was a strong ciggy, or so I thought, from the pack of *Rothman's Special Mild Red* I stole from my mother. I can still taste the sulphur of the match next to the cold wind on my cheek. The first time I tried, I started coughing, but continued since I felt like a badass. At last—I felt *something*, and I liked it. It felt good to inhale and exhale those little O-rings in the air, almost like saying, "F**k you, World," with every exhaled "O."

In those moments, I'd found a partner for loneliness. That partner's name was anger. My newly found persona was a gift, but it also became a curse. I grew angry with a protective shell, just like Rachel had. I really had no choice; I was hurting and was confused about what might be wrong with me. I began hating myself, hating my body, hating my mind, and hating my life. It was all my fault, or so I thought.

Children are naturally egocentric, which is a normal part of development. Consequently, this results in children assuming they are at fault when something negative occurs. There is always a message in every behaviour we demonstrate. Whether it be a mother who yells at her child, or a thirteen year-old smoking stolen cigarettes; there is a reason. My reason, as I mentioned, stemmed from confusion about being lonely, which led me to anger; the best and most dangerous of any protective layer (more on this in later chapters). I'll share this with you though: Anger is the guard for hurt. It's an important part of coping and grieving. But if you let it hang around, it'll do damage.

Rachel ended up at a private school and burned many bridges, or so I heard from her school friends. I still think of her often, and wish I could reach out to her. Unfortunately, in my profession, we can't do that. Not knowing how things turn out is a hard part of being a therapist. We too feel hope for our clients and love seeing them succeed. Either way, the money and lavish lifestyle Rachel had did not help her in any way. Wealth, like any other "void fillers" can be a bandaid which will slowly fall off and expose the injury. You can take meds, have a stiff drink, smoke a joint, and all will numb the pain for a bit. But the pain eventually comes back. And, you can take your mind off it for a bit, look at some porn, gamble your life savings away, but your mind will find its way back to your challenges. The void first needs to be nurtured and cared for. Only then will it heal. If you want to keep your destructive habits from recurring, you must keep the void close and stay connected. Over the next few chapters, you will learn how to do this, which can change the trajectory of your future, and all relationships in your path.

I wouldn't change a thing about my childhood. You might say it was my destiny from which I learned a great deal. It has given me the ability to understand both loneliness and emotional fulfilment. Living it has given me the ability to understand the sneaky void that pops-up once in a while, along with my pesky "Anxiety;" the monster who gets triggered by the void. By understanding these things about myself and my development, I am more confident in relationships and in myself. But, I continue to be a work in progress. By understanding my childhood experiences, I am able to be emotionally connected and bonded with my loved ones. Plus, I can relate to the many people who share the same challenges I did. So, I really know who I am. And you can too!

Let's start at the beginning by thinking about your values and standards. We all have differences of opinions, beliefs, and thoughts that impact the way we are in relationships. Take some time to figure this out about yourself. Not only will it allow you to get in touch with who you are, but it will also help guide you towards healing voids that may be present. Understanding who you are can be an empowering moment in your life. Being aware of your values and standards will allow you to really appreciate who you are and who you strive to be. Knowing them will also help you ensure you don't compromise your values.

So, do you know your values and standards? What about your partner's values? Are they aligned with yours? For example, values could include honesty, generosity, or even religious beliefs. A standard, also known as a non-negotiable, can include rules in your home, telling your partner everything involving your children, and having dinner at the table. I encourage you to take a moment to make a list of your values and standards. You may surprise yourself! Throughout this book, you will notice boxes with the words, "My Bold & Brave Diary." When we write down our thoughts, beliefs, emotions, and feelings, they feel much more real and tangible. In essence, you are bringing those things to the forefront or into being. Often, it can be scary to put these onto paper. Remember, you can always cross them out and change your answers. You can return to it when you are finished reading this book as well. We are always evolving and will continue to be works in progress. So, the question is: Will you be daring with me and put your thoughts on paper? I know you really don't want to; I get it. But you are the one that bought the book, and are wanting change in your relationships. So, can you complete just one question to start? That would be one step towards the right direction!

My Bold & Brave Diary...

Values and Standards:

One thing I know about myself is...

_____

_____

_____

A non negotiable for me in my home/life/relationships is...

_____

_____

_____

Something I really value about myself/my family/my life is...

_____

_____

_____

I don't have any values and standards but will start a list here:

_____

_____

_____

THE BOTTOM LINE UNFILTERED...

This book is not about what people have or have not done to me; it's about my own experiences and how they impacted me. And by extension, it's about the experiences that you've had and how they've impacted you as well. There are many variables that can impact how we perceive experiences, and how they affect us in the present and future. My childhood may be looked at differently from the eyes of my siblings, but they are not me. I have always been labelled as overly sensitive, weak, with a small capacity for tough stuff because I become emotional. And of course, I have been defined by the five-letter word I hate: *needy*. But, today, I have a completely different view of myself; I see myself as *strong* since I feel emotions. Think about it: if being emotional and feeling deeply is a sign of weakness, then what would the sign of strength be? Not feeling anything? Holding it in? Shutting down and not talking about it? Umm, that's easy to answer, isn't it? So, do you agree that this means the true hard thing to do is to be vulnerable and share your emotions with your loved ones? Allow my journey to be an access point for you. How do my universal experiences parallel what you're going through? Though you may not have had parents who owned a restaurant, maybe you've felt lonely, inadequate, small, or useless. We stand together. We can learn together.

So, I know who I am: an emotional being with strengths that I can share in my job, as a mother, a wife, and a therapist. But I also know what I am not: I am not always calm like I want to be, I can't cook well, but have learned to laugh at myself most of the time. I am terrible with time and get upset at myself for being notoriously late. And I don't know how to stop sweating the small stuff. I also know that I will never be adventurous like Indiana Jones, or have legs like Tina Turner. And I will never, ever, be able to jump off the back of a boat to join others who are snorkelling in the ocean, like my husband can. Just the thought of that makes my stomach turn. I have learned these things over the last 45 years, by experiencing trial and error, grace and cruelty, resilience and frailness. There is still a list of things I have trouble accepting about myself, and am working on. Some, I am too scared to work on. Sometimes our fear tricks us into believing it keeps us safe. But I will get there.

The question is: Are you ready to get there too? The writing exercises in this book are meant to help you do just that; to work on self acceptance. The writing prompts will help you gain insight into your patterns, cycles, and will allow you to learn about yourself well beyond the surface level.

Remember, your past does not have to dictate who you are today. Your life and your experiences are not your fault, but they are your responsibility! Can you leave your experiences behind, learn from them, and move on?

If you need support to do this, seek therapy, seek support from a friend you trust; and read chapter 2. Next, you will learn about *attachment* and why you may be having a difficult time moving forward. For now, let's start with you writing down your thoughts about who you are and who you are not. Do you accept yourself? Take some time to think about this and make a list below. If you really can't stand the writing portions of this book, just take a moment to think about the questions. Record your answer with speech to text, make a video for yourself to hold yourself accountable, tell your Golden Retriever, dream about it, but quit your bitchin' and for Pete's sake, just do something that will start the process with me!

My Bold & Brave Diary...

Who are you?

_____

_____

_____

Who are you not?

_____

_____

_____

Have you accepted this about yourself?

_____

_____

_____

_____

What have you not accepted about yourself? Are you ready to work on it?

_____

_____

_____

_____

Key takeaways:

1. The unwanted behaviours that may be destructive are symptoms of something much deeper, such as a void caused by loneliness.

2. Learn who you are and who you aren't, so you can accept yourself. Work on what you can't accept. Accept who you will never be.

CHAPTER TWO

Attachment

WARNING: THIS CHAPTER'S ANECDOTE
MAY TRIGGER READERS WITH A HISTORY
OF CHILDHOOD PHYSICAL ABUSE.

*"Let's talk about the new AI-artificial intimacy.
We have 1,000 friends on social, but we don't have
a single person who can feed our cat for us."*

—ESTHER PEREL—

Now that we have an understanding of how we may feel a void, it's helpful to understand *why* we feel it. As mentioned in chapter one, we all experience life differently. What we bring to relationships differs based on what has happened to us, how we interpret experiences, and many other variables. How we approach our loved ones and respond to their emotions (or lack of), depends on our own attachments; in other words, our relationships of the past. Attachment refers to a connection with another person; early attachment generally refers to the relationship with our caregiver, which most often represents our first relationship. *Attachment Theory*, developed by psychiatrist John Bowlby, suggests that our early relationship with parents or caregivers shapes our behavior in later relationships. That is, the experience of the first relationship with our caregiver creates a template and structure for our future relationships. It teaches how to interpret relationships and establishes the status quo for expectations and our behaviour. Unfortunately, this can be the case for both positive relationships and neglectful relationships between caregiver and child. This can create confusion, lack of safety, and a very negative internal feeling about ourselves, since children internalize negative treatment from others.

We also create an understanding of ourselves in relationships early on, which becomes a part of our own narrative and can influence who we choose to be with, how we act, respond, and interpret things as adults. What you like and what you don't like can also be influenced by your upbringing, past relationships, and, of course, your own tastes. From this narrative, also known as the *internal working model of self,* we view our relationships from the perspective of this internal working model, using the same lens every time. Metaphorically, one can appreciate that if we're seeing life through a broken or dirty set of glasses, the view won't change until the glasses are replaced or cleaned. So, we are given a message when we are little ones that we carry with us throughout our lives. This message can be positive or negative and gives us a so-called framework about future relationships and how they may play out. The viewpoint acts like a prediction of how any relationship will unfold based on the primary relationship's experience. Since we all experience these relationships differently, the ways in which we respond and cope with events in our lives will reflect our experiences and perceptions.

More often than not, it is our childhood experiences that formulate our present day habits and predilections. As a child, we are either taught that relationships are safe, or unpredictable and dangerous, which is often based on the experiences we have with our direct caregivers. If you were loved and nurtured as a child, then you would have a different perspective on relationships than someone who was mistreated as a child. How we attach or un-attach ourselves to our caregivers as children makes an impact on us that we carry into adulthood and often formulates our relationship patterns. Now, this doesn't mean we're broken if our parents were terrible to us; it means that we may have some work to do and may need some help healing. In this chapter we are learning about *insecure* attachment. But in later chapters, we will learn about *secure* attachment and how to get ourselves there.

It wasn't until I understood attachment and how it applies to my life that I was able to move past the weight of the word "needy" that I mentioned in chapter one. Bowlby's theory of attachment espouses that the earliest bonds children form with their caregivers has a significant impact that continues throughout life. These early experiences manifest through our behaviour in relationships and our belief system that was created as our primary caregivers loved, avoided, or neglected us.

I'll ask you to reflect for a moment and ask yourself if you were neglected, abused, or mistreated by the adult who was supposed to love and nurture you as the helpless child you were. Children often tend to internalize the faults of a caregiver and internalize the hurt that comes with being ignored by their parents. Unconsciously, children tend to see their parents as perfect, and themselves as flawed.

Oh, if I try harder, maybe mommy will notice me!

When Mom doesn't notice, the child continues to try harder or internalizes a reality that Mommy doesn't want to be with them.

My mommy doesn't like me. She won't spend time with me and play.

The child interprets these implicit messages by believing they, themselves, are flawed. As a result, the child reasons that the parent does not want to spend time with them. And as a consequence, the child's attachment style starts to develop insecurely. They become protective of their own emotions since they can sense their caregiver is not attuned to them. *Attunement* is the ability to tend to a child's needs. This starts from the womb and is critical during the first five years of life. Children can sense when a situation feels unsafe. As a result, children will often self-censor themselves if it doesn't feel safe to share their emotions with their caregiver. If the caregiver is preoccupied and not able to be attentive to the child, the emotional safety will not be there and the child will usually pick up on this. Therefore, the lack of emotional safety continues until a new experience of safely sharing and receiving emotions a.k.a. attunement is experienced in a consistent way. However, the new learned experiences take a lot longer to undo than the ease with which the habits were formed in the first place. This generally does not happen until adulthood, after some self exploration, self awareness work and often, some psychotherapy to assist in seeing the patterns that show up in relationships.

Now, this does not mean we need to be attentive to our children every waking minute. After all, it isn't what we do for our children but what we teach them to do for themselves that makes all the difference. It's about creating emotional safety by being present, being dependable and accountable. (More on this in later chapters when we learn about secure attachment.) But for now, let's continue by examining insecure attachment styles.

There are three main types of insecure attachment styles:

1. Anxious (or preoccupied; referred to as anxious ambivalent in children)
2. Avoidant (or dismissive; referred to as anxious avoidant in children)
3. Disorganized (or fearful; referred to as fearful avoidant in children)

Do you know if your caregiver loved you very much? Did they do their best but weren't able to be present, figuratively or literally? Perhaps one of your parents was in the military and had to serve overseas. Maybe they were a doctor or a nurse who had to work night shifts or travel. Or, were you scared of your caregiver? This would make your caregiver both a source of safety and fear, since you had no choice but to rely on them for the basic necessities of life. Perhaps your caregiver was kind and loving to you but was very preoccupied. We see this a lot in today's society given the enormous hours most adults must commit to work in order to make ends meet. Whichever way, each attachment style has a very predictable behavioural response, which produces a predictable cycle in relationships.

When you begin to understand the insecure attachment styles, awareness allows us to begin to understand our own styles. However, the problem with insecure attachment styles is that they will never go away on their own. This is why healing our insecurities is key to achieving a secure relationship. As a bandaid, many will try to seek affection or continue to avoid and push their negative feelings down deep. But if we don't heal from our attachment injuries, we will carry them into our adulthood which can damage every relationship we encounter.

ANXIOUS INSECURE ATTACHMENT

The anxious and insecurely attached person will seem preoccupied, perhaps overly clingy, be complementary to others, and may even belittle themselves. They are often very fearful of abandonment and rejection; which can also lead to jealousy, envy and excessive behaviours with their partner. Do you remember Rachel from chapter one? Her experience was like half the clients I encounter. She demonstrated traits of an anxiously attached person. Her clinginess and self sabotaging behaviour was synonymous with an anxious attachment. Rachel was not physically harmed by her mother, but experienced emotional harm which caused a void within her. The void should have been occupied by a deep, emotional connection with her mother. Instead, her mother was far from being attuned and did not notice Rachel's emotions as she was growing up. Due to Rachel's experience as a child, where she continually tried to have her needs met, but never quite had them satisfied, an anxious attachment was created within her. Now, perhaps circumstances prevented Rachel's mother from being attuned to Rachel. This is not meant to put blame on our caregivers. However, the proof is in the behaviour of the child. Rachel grew up to have unmet needs as a result of her experiences as a young child.

Please break for a moment and ask yourself, "Does this resonate with me?" What this means is that the anxiously attached person will work hard to get noticed but the "noticing" will never be good enough. Some will strive for perfection, so that they can get accolades in order to be noticed. Some will become people pleasers, high achievers, and may see others as more valuable than themselves. Anxious attachment clients also make themselves extra busy, and can not leave space in the schedule to just "be." They are constantly "doing." By keeping busy, they don't have to think about the void. The on-the-go person may even struggle to stop and relax. In fact, the notion of relaxation may seem like a foreign concept to those with an insecure attachment style. Who wouldn't want to relax on the couch and do nothing, right? But for the anxiously attached, this can present as a stressful activity. "Being still" instead of "doing" is an important concept to master. Not only does it allow space for emotions to come up, but it can also highlight what's going on around you that might be missed. Do you remember the character in the Charlie Brown cartoon, Pigpen, who moved around with a dust cloud around him? If he were to stop, the dust would settle on him. He may feel the weight of the world. Imagine running a race, and abruptly stopping. All of a sudden, you would feel your heart rate more intensely, your breath would become more obvious, and you may even experience a tingly sensation. It is very difficult to stop mid run, since the momentum focuses you and propels you forward. If you stop, you lose that. The anxiously attached person will have been very preoccupied most of their life, just like Pigpen or a runner.

Generally, an anxiously attached person will also have experienced moments that have translated into a negative perception of self, resulting in an insatiable desire to work hard in order to prove something. This can reflect itself in an inner or outer way. An anxiously attached person will continue to experience this cycle until they learn about themselves and heal from the effects of not being noticed as a child. As mentioned above, that lack of attention, especially in a child, means that their needs weren't being met, oftentimes due to the fact that either their parents' work schedules weren't conducive to family time, or in some cases because that's the way parents raised their children in a different era, time, or set of conditions. Have you ever heard someone say, "Oh, they just do that for attention!"? Damn right they do! They are trying to fill their unmet needs; but unfortunately, no amount of attention will suffice. However, there are ways to fill the void and become securely attached. More on that in a later chapter.

There are multiple reasons why a parent or caregiver cannot be emotionally present. We must understand this if we're to move forward and heal. Perhaps your parent experienced horrible trauma from their own childhood and never learned that it was safe to open up emotional channels to their children. That's only one example, but there are an abundance of reasons for parents being emotionally unavailable. Regardless, this is not a blame game. Rather, understanding attachment and how you fit within the various styles will give you insight into patterns and habits that may be doing damage to your relationships and to yourself. Often an anxious attachment within oneself can create low self esteem or a fear of rejection, which can manifest as being "clingy" in relationships.

You may even have developed a maladaptive coping mechanism in your primary relationships that prevent positive interactions with your partner. Again, I will drive home the point that why you do what you do is completely understandable when you comprehend attachment styles. The uncomfortable emotions are what you are fighting, which should make total sense as you grasp these concepts. Remember: this is what you were taught and what you learned at a young age. Emotions are often hard to feel for those who've been raised by someone who couldn't provide an emotional channel. Naturally, this would make someone feel uncomfortable when it comes to any display of emotion. The consequence being that while you may have done a good job of protecting yourself throughout your life from the uncomfortable emotions, your pattern is now constricting your relationship. Think about that phrase: Your pattern is now constricting your relationship. In other words, it's being strangled or cut off. Unpleasant, right? It is not your fault that this happened to you at a very young age. It simply means that you have lived with an understanding that relationships are not safe. It also means that it *is* your responsibility to heal from it, so you can have a secure attachment within your relationships.

Please break for another moment and consider how wonderful it would be to not worry about your relationships the way you do now; to know that your partner has your back no matter what happens. What emotion runs through you when you take the time to consider that possibility? Because I will tell you definitively that it is possible to feel secure.

AVOIDANT INSECURE ATTACHMENT

The second insecure attachment style is an *avoidant* style, wherein the main coping mechanism involves avoiding anything related to emotions. The maladaptive coping skill of shutting down to avoid feeling anything emotional, contributes to that which is intended to be suppressed. The consequence is that the suppressed emotion only gets stronger on the inside. Sometimes, avoiders will "blow up" after a long hiatus of not showing up in discussion and experiencing their emotions. These adults have been taught, from a young age, that what they are feeling, may not be important, may not matter, or is not safe to share. Children who have adopted this attachment style generally have a caregiver who expects them to be self-sufficient emotionally and "tough" by not showing emotions. The irony is that the reverse is true. Like I mentioned in chapter I, holding in your emotions is often seen as the easy route. Although, holding one's emotions in can create havoc inside your body: blood pressure can be affected, and so can the central nervous system.

Avoiders are thought of as not wanting the connection when, in fact, the opposite is true: They *want* connection but are scared of it. Often, an avoider may feel like it is a weakness to share emotions and be vulnerable. Unconsciously terrified of connecting, they bring their unsafe childlike-state experiences to their modern day situations. Avoidant attachers are taught to take care of their own emotional needs instead of relying on others. As adults, these children will continue to appear confident and self-sufficient, almost like "loners" in life, often with a positive view of themselves but a negative one of others. This makes it difficult for them to form secure relationships, oftentimes with an avoidance of physical intimacy. Their go-to coping skill is to shut down and flee; they protect themselves from the uncomfortable emotions this way. Coping with the blocked emotions often results in addictions or other unhealthy behaviours which may alleviate or numb the feeling for a moment, only to have it come back more intensely. It becomes a cycle that fosters more addictive habits and a relentless mission to block the emotions. The numbing feeling that may come from addictive behaviour is always fleeting and never lasts.

You will read more about attachment in the remaining chapters, and how it influences actions (or inactions) in relationships. As well, we will explore how to heal from these attachments and how to change them into a secure attachment.

So, that little child is still within you, as mentioned in chapter 1. Your inner child continues to hurt and feel refused, unloved, and may have a belief that they will never be good enough. Take a moment to reflect and ask yourself, "What is my inner child feeling? What is my own inner narrative?"

DISORGANIZED INSECURE ATTACHMENT

As children, *disorganized (fearful)* attached individuals will often be unpredictable in their behaviour, will not speak up about needing help, and may seem self sufficient. All of these traits may be signs of an inability to form secure bonds. Some children (and adults) may engage in risky behaviour, substances, or may be removed from any emotional opportunity to connect. They may have been taught, through the actions/inactions of their caregiver, that they can't rely on them for their needs. As well, they have a hard time adapting to their caregiver since their caregiver's behaviour is often unpredictable. Risky behaviour, substance abuse, and mental health struggles stemming from trauma, are often a result of this kind of childhood. A disorganized (fearful) attachment is often thought of as a blend of the other two (anxious and avoidant) and is a difficult one to identify clearly. The story of Jordan is one of an insecure disorganized attachment style...

THE STORY OF JORDAN

Jordan came to me asking for some help with his relationship. His girlfriend was on the verge of leaving him if he didn't get some support. He really didn't understand why his girlfriend continually told him to figure out what was wrong. Jordan avoided anything that related to feelings or emotions, which according to Jordan, meant that he wasn't bothered by anything. When I started working with Jordan, we talked about his history. He was very nonchalant when sharing his experiences as a child. Jordan was young, around 20 years old, and had never talked to a therapist before. He had just moved out of his mother's home where he had lived most of his life. For him, having a single mom was the norm since he was seven years old when his father left.

You know, my dad left and I was okay with it. He wasn't very nice to be around. He was pretty grumpy and drank a lot. I remember him getting mad quite often and walking on eggshells around him because if he got mad—watch out. But I guess that's what fathers are supposed to do, right?

Well, every father is different and it's important to understand if your father provided you with the nurturing and love a young boy would require. Did he?

I don't know, he worked a lot. Isn't that love? He taught me right from wrong. If I disrespected him, he hit me. I remember this one time he kicked me down the stairs.

What? How old were you?

Oh, I was probably only four years old. I stole a chocolate bar from his drawer beside his chair. He always had so many snacks in that drawer. I didn't think he would notice. I just remember thinking, 'Why are you so angry? It's just a chocolate bar.' But, man, he was so angry.

Where was your mother when this happened?

Oh, she was there too. She told me I should have respected my dad's belongings. It was all my fault that he got mad and kicked me down the stairs. I was black and blue for days. I guess I deserved it.

If you had your own little boy now, would you kick him down the stairs for stealing a chocolate bar from you?

Hell no.

Tell me why not.

Well it seems barbaric, really. I mean, what's that going to teach the kid? But I never really thought of it that way before. I always just remember feeling like I deserved it.

Jordan, you did not deserve it, and your dad kicking you down the stairs was about your dad losing control of his own emotions and losing control of his body. He was the one who was out of control and *acting in a completely inappropriate, abusive way towards a young child. It **was** barbaric and it had nothing to do with you because his anger was about him and his own issues that he carried. He could have been arrested for this. There was nothing you could do, that would provoke a father to do that to his child. Children make mistakes and need to be taught how to fix them. An appropriate thing for a father to do would be to explain that it is not right to steal. Instead, he should have taught you how to apologize, then moved on. Being kicked down the stairs is about your father's anger and not being able to control it. It is not meant to teach anything; it's only a display of a violent man who behaved terribly to his son.*

All I learned from him is that I was a piece of s**t. And I still feel that way.

Jordan began to sob.

I am so sorry this happened to you and to that little boy.

Jordan and I did some work around his experiences as a little boy. When Jordan would try to get his father's attention, he would be shut down with words that created fear within him. Jordan's earliest memory of this is when he was so proud of a picture he drew for his dad at school, and came home to give it to him. Instead of showing interest in the picture, which is what an attuned father would do, Jordan heard, "I'm busy" instead. Jordan crumpled up his picture and threw it under his bed. Although this may seem like a small moment in the life of an adult, it was a pivotal one in Jordan's little brain.

Children who have a caregiver such as Jordan's father often develop a fearful/disorganized attachment style. It's often considered the most difficult attachment style from which to heal. Jordan's father was supposed to be a source of safety, but instead he was a source of fear. Jordan's earliest experience in relationships taught him to be fearful and on guard. As a result, he realized it was safer to shut down, and not to show his emotions as a child. Often, this is when we will see a child act out or become very angry. Remember, children ask for help in the most unattractive ways. Thus his experience became a part of him and any conflict cycle in his adult relationships.

Quick Tip:

Take a moment, close your eyes, and imagine yourself as a child. Are you able to look at your younger self with love in your eyes? Can you take your child-self's hand and tell them you will take care of them? Or are you filled with disgust and shame? Or perhaps you can't visualize yourself at the moment. Continue this exercise for the next few nights, when you're ready to go to sleep and your home is quiet. Notice any changes as the evenings pass...

It is not until you can release and heal this negative inner model of self that you will truly see that, no matter how you behaved, it was the adult's role to nurture and love you unconditionally. I will say this again: The adult is responsible if they didn't do this. 100%. YOU were an innocent child. YOU were the one who required love, care, and nurturing that your caregiver(s) would not or could not provide. YOU are the victim here of a false narrative, that you have been carrying your entire life. So, are you ready to get rid of this? Or perhaps you had a caring, nurturing caregiver who couldn't provide the emotional connection based on life's circumstances. Are you able to forgive them? Are you able to look at them from an adult lens and say, "You were loving and did the best you could"?

You have the capability to do this. It is also your responsibility to do this. It's your time. In later chapters, we will work on this and will learn how to heal from these attachment injuries. But first, we must understand what attachment style stands out for you and how it plays a role in the cycle you may have within your relationships. Before moving to chapter three, have a look at the chart below. Do any of these resonate with you? Perhaps you feel like you are securely attached, which would make you a very lucky human! Or, perhaps you haven't recognized some of your patterns. Either way, keep an open mind, and read on...

In a nutshell:

1.   We develop an attachment style based on what's happened to us in our lives, and we unconsciously create an inner narrative. That is, an inner working model of ourselves, our perception of who we are and how we operate.
2.   We may feel uncomfortable emotions because of the inner narrative.
3.   We act a certain way (fight/flee) to protect ourselves from the uncomfortable emotions.
4.   The protection (fight/flee) constricts our relationship by not allowing a secure emotional bond, which is too scary for our unconscious mind.

The following resource can be found at the end of the book as well, to go back to as you read through this book:

Common Characteristics of Attachment Styles
Note: This is not a diagnostic assessment, but a guide to help identify which attachment style to explore further.

ATTACH-MENT TYPE	Anxious:	Avoidant:	Disorganized:
	• I am often preoccupied, overbooked, not attuned or present in the conversation. • I often belittle myself openly and will lift others up in excess. • I need constant reassurance from my partner. • Emotions are scary and intense.	• I may seem uninterested in anything remotely serious or may crack many jokes to avoid being uncomfortable. • I often will change the subject if faced with conversations about emotions. • I may belittle or dismiss others to avoid all emotional engagement. • Emotions are uncomfortable and gross.	• I may seem avoidant at times or may dismiss others. • I may belittle others and their emotions. but could also seem genuinely interested. • If I was interested, it would stop there. I would not be attuned to others. • Emotions are scary and uncomfortable.
WHY	• I had an unavailable, preoccupied parent/caregiver.	• I had a strict, emotionally absent parent/caregiver.	• I had a traumatic childhood and/or an abusive parent. • My parent/caregiver was scary and unpredictable.

CHARACTER-ISTICS	• I have a negative view of myself but a positive view of others. • I have an intense fear of rejection and abandonment. • I can be "clingy" in relationships. • I often feel unworthy of love.	• I have a positive view of myself and often a negative view of others. • I tend to reject others before they can reject themselves • I am often closed off	• I have a negative view of myself and a negative view of others. • I can include both anxious and avoidant characteristics. • I am often unpredictable with my emotions.
BEHAVIOUR (protection from uncomfortable feelings)	• I will pursue arguments or conflicts to prove my point or get my way. • I seek validation from my partner often. • I will continually ask for help if I need it and won't stop until I get what I think I need which is to be validated/recognized. • I often overshare personal information to others.	• I will shut down when faced with conflict, often will default to the flight response. • I will avoid being vulnerable and intimate. • I will seem independent and self-reliant. I've been known as a "loner" who beats to my own drum. • I will downplay emotions, and dismiss others. • I won't ask for help since it is a weakness.	• I'll have a difficult time trusting anyone. • I know I need my partner but I often want them to go away, but then want them back, then to go away...etc... • It feels scary to get close to anyone.

Are the majority of boxes ticked off in a certain column? Perhaps it isn't obvious if you have adopted an insecure attachment. Perhaps you are a combination of each. Either way, the information in chapter two is meant as an educational tool for you to think about. It can be very helpful to understand the "why" behind our patterns in relationships. I have often heard, "Why are my relationships always ending this way?" Or, "Why do I always pick the wrong person?" Well, this is where understanding attachment comes in handy. Behaviours become predictable, along with our interactions, which informs what we choose to have in our lives.

THE BOTTOM LINE UNFILTERED...

As I mentioned in the beginning of this chapter, insecure attachment styles can be healed and new securely attached bonds can be formed. With some hard work, emotional openness, and vulnerability (all the scary stuff), the healing becomes attainable. The brain is malleable. That is, we can create new pathways and neural networks. The part of the brain that perceives abandonment is the most neuroplastic area! That means you can heal from it as long as you have consistent attachment and safety while doing the healing work. A certified therapist can help you uncover some of the hurt you may have from your past. This can be a necessary step to excavate the deep emotions that have been weighing you down. As you do this work, you may also wonder about other important aspects of your relationship. Did you learn what "normal" is from your caregiver? Or is your way a maladaptive approach? Perhaps you have certain ideals that have not been working. For example, are you approaching your relationship 50/50? (Meaning, everything must be split?) Or maybe you believe that there are manly jobs that only men do. (Insert eye roll here.) Don't worry: we're going to look at the roles in relationships that could be impacting your emotional connection. In the next chapter, we will uncover some relationship roles that may make you think twice about how you view your role in your relationship.

Key takeaways:

1. Your past is not your fault, but it is your responsibility to work through.
2. Insecure attachment styles can be healed to form a secure attachment style.
3. Learn how to "be" instead of always "doing".
4. Behaviour in a relationship is a reflection of what's inside of us and our past experiences.

CHAPTER THREE

Relationship Roles

"If your significant other is mad at you, put a cape on them and say, 'Now you're super mad!' If they laugh, marry them."

—ANONYMOUS—

I wasn't sure how to write parts of this book about relationships and how to have hope on days when I couldn't muster a drop of it myself. Like all of you, we have days that are total stress, when we just need a night off to relax and figure out how to cope. Whether it's a cigarette or an Amazon purchase, we cope in various ways. I was having more of those days than I wanted. I let a few months go by before I even opened the manuscript to this very book you're reading. I couldn't face it, it was just another thing to add to my to-do list. And I thought, *how am I supposed to write about being hopeful, when I don't have an ounce of hope myself?* Then it dawned on me that this is how *you* may feel. This is how my clients feel. So it can and should be in print, for all to read. I put my pen to paper, like 1901, and started scratching out notes about being stuck in a hopeless cycle, in January, in the frigid cold, feeling undesirable, overtired, and anxious as hell. Yes, my friends, therapists can be basketcases too. Often, we are the worst! We often choose to help others very well, instead of ourselves.

Have you heard of vicarious trauma? It's a form of trauma that happens when we witness trauma, either by seeing or hearing about it. It's somewhat common amongst therapists and certainly amongst paramedics, fire fighters, police, and other service providers like teachers and business leaders. But it can manifest for just about anyone. It certainly did for me. I literally have felt my body shift from being ok to this weird, gremlin like thing in my body, taking up space. I either have to fly the coop, freeze, faint, or fight it. Fortunately, I can feel it when it's coming so I try to ground myself in the moment so that I'm not overtaken by the trauma (and don't turn into a gremlin).

Instead, I am able to continue being the helper I committed to being in my work; but oftentimes find myself dealing with the trauma later. It gets stuck in the limbic system of the brain, and is overloaded with jumbled information that will continually show up if I don't deal with it. The sooner we deal with trauma, the better. So, I will usually talk with my therapist as soon as possible. I will cry and I will try to be ok. None of this, of course, makes all the other moments in my life stop while I deal with what's at hand. Whenever I have an episode, I need to face my family and I still need to be a mom and a wife. However, it is in those moments, that we most need support from our loved ones. That's the weird thing about any form of trauma. It's not the actual event, but the emotional experience that can leave you feeling overwhelmed, unsafe, and helpless. This emotional experience left alone, isolated, and not comforted, creates the trauma within your body. The lack of support after an event can exacerbate the distress that creates the trauma. If we receive support following a bad event, we're more likely to be able to process it safely and it won't take up real estate in our limbic system of the brain. But when we don't have that comforting support or we choose/default to shut down and not seek support, we store the bad event along with a negative thought about ourselves. This is one of the reasons trauma sticks; the negative thought fosters terrible feelings that can keep us immobilized, unable to cope and constantly triggered. This affects our relationships, amongst a long list of other elements in our lives.

I often hear how couples shut down, are silent for days, haven't had sex in months, or are sleeping in separate rooms. Many are alone when things around them are status quo, and they are really alone when traumatic events arise. How does one cope on their own without a team? Maybe a little help from Jack Daniels? Excessive work? Or maybe compulsive shopping or exercising? (Yes, that is an avoidance tactic too.) Or are they asking for help? In my experience as a therapist, the three words that people have the most difficult time saying are, "I need help." Why? Doesn't everyone need help? Why is needing help synonymous with being weak, in the minds of many? It has a negative connotation and often the one who asks for help is regarded as being helpless or needy (cringe). Remember, it's "safer" to go it alone, not ask for help and shut down. But it's **hard** to ask for help. Let me say that again, saying those three words are not for the faint of heart!

Can you say them? I know you can. I'll even do it with you.

I. NEED. HELP.

Feeling stuck is a tough place to land. Like sands through the hourglass, so are the days of our lives...whoops! I mean, like sand stuck in an hourglass, sometimes you want to push a big stick into it and light the end on fire. KABOOM! Let's blow that out and get unstuck. Allow me to share a few ways that may help you. But first let's look at what happened to Tyra and Simon.

THE STORY OF TYRA & SIMON

Tyra was a sweet, anxiously attached, overachiever who spent her life planning her next step, next meal, and next fart. It was excessive. She planned and planned, which on the outside, may have looked like she had her s**t together, and it didn't stink either. The overwhelming need to plan and be planned stemmed from her anxiety, which included worries about her husband's health, his job, and his drive to get a better job. She felt that she was being helpful in planning life for the unhappy couple. This is why she was so confused when her partner, Simon, would give her attitude when she brought up the more senior job opportunity that had recently come up at his work.

I don't understand! I'm just trying to help! He's so great at what he does and is very capable of moving up to the next level. I don't get it! I mean why doesn't he just listen to me? It hurts, you know. I have some great ideas and he just rolls his eyes at me and then goes to the garage.

I see. So Tyra, I am hearing that you are frustrated and feeling unheard and not validated, correct?

Yes, I just said that. You aren't listening either.

Ok, Tyra, I am listening and paraphrasing what you're saying to make sure I'm getting it right. So often, we send messages other than what we're saying. I don't want to discount the message you're trying to get across. Explicit messages can be described well through

*words, but implicit messages can be interpreted a number of ways.
Do you agree?*

*Well, yes, I guess so. But isn't it obvious that I just want the best
for him?*

*I don't know if it's obvious to him. You have shared how much you
love Simon and want this relationship to persevere. Is it ok if I ask
him how he feels, right now?*

Tyra looked confused. In EFT couples therapy sessions, we
work with each partner individually, with the other... This back-
and-forth process helps identify the negative communication
cycle, which we'll explore further in the next chapter.

*Simon, when you hear Tyra explain how she is feeling, what does
that bring up for you?*

I can't understand her. She's so annoying. Someti–

*Simon, can we slow down for a moment? Let's just go a little slower.
I am looking for an emotion, not what you are thinking. An emotion.*

Simon looked confused. Men typically have three emotions:
sad, mad, and glad. This was an opportunity for some coaching.

Simon, do you feel anything in your body as we slow down?

Yes.

Ok, tell me.

I feel like I want to puke.

Ok, that can't feel good. I wonder...if there could be any nervous feelings...or anxiety in your body?

No, I'm just pissed off.

Sure. I understand. You're pissed off, and I wonder if you see Tyra's comments in a different way than how she meant them?

Well, they sound condescending. I know she meant it that way!

Ok, tell me more.

When I hear her say things like, "go apply for a better job" or "we need to make more money," all I can think of is—well I get pissed off.

Ok, stay with me, all I can think of is.....?

Well, I said, I'm angry!

Ok Simon, can you go underneath the anger for a moment? I am curious what else is there.

He looked away and said, *I am not good enough.* In a very low voice.

Ok, that must have been really hard to say, Simon. Thank you for sharing. How do you feel saying this out loud to Tyra?

I feel ashamed.

Ok,

Tyra interjected and said, *"What? Why? You shouldn't feel like that; you're amaz-*

Tyra, let's give Simon some space for these difficult emotions he is sharing.

This is a crucial point in discussions, when our loved ones share how they are feeling. If we attempt to "make" them feel better, we fail to validate them. Even if they are feeling like Simon did, they still need validation of their feelings. It isn't about whether you agree or disagree with the statement. This is about *their* feelings.

Simon, you don't feel good enough. I am so sorry you feel this way. Can you tell me more?

Sure, when Tyra says things like, "go get a better job," or when she tells me what I should do in general, it feels like she doesn't think I'm capable. Like she doesn't have faith in me. I hate it. Almost like I'm a kid again.

Ok, this sounds very frustrating for you. To feel like a child in the relationship...?

Yes, it's like my mom is talking to me.

And there it was. At last, Simon figured it out. He shared that he does not want to be mothered by his girlfriend, which was clearly happening. More on this in the next section.

So, we have discovered how you interact in a relationship with your partner, and what you were taught growing up about relationships. But what are your thoughts on your role in your current relationship? Below, I have outlined some important factors that may help you in your relationship roles. Also, they may give you insight into understanding how your partner may be feeling or what they're facing. Either way, our end goal is to have compassion and understanding for one another so we can stay out of the way and let the different roles flourish.

STOP PARENTING YOUR PARTNER

Simon shared that he felt like Tyra was mothering him by telling him what to do. By dictating what she thought he should do, even in a loving way, she was "mothering" her partner. A total no-no if you want your relationship to work. Simon had a mommy. He didn't need another one. So, the first tip to take with you from this chapter is to stop mothering/fathering/parenting your partner. Stop it. It's condescending and disrespectful. Your partner is a big boy/girl/person for that matter, and they need to learn how to to adult, if they haven't already. If you keep mothering them, they won't learn. Instead, they'll stay where they're at and will resent you. Instead, be supportive by listening. Perhaps ask your partner if they want your help. Remind them you are there for them.

START VALIDATING YOUR PARTNER

What would happen if you said to your partner, "I'm really struggling here, and I just need you with me. I don't want to talk, I just need you to be present with me"? I wonder how it would end if you stayed in the discomfort of needing help?

Oftentimes, there's a hidden source of power in the safe examination of that which causes us the most discomfort. How would this newfound strength impact your relationship?

I want you to imagine a small window, which represents our tolerance for facing hard stuff and feeling the discomfort of tough emotions. Every time we face this, our window will open a bit. *The window of tolerance* is a term that refers to what a person can tolerate before being pushed "over the edge" (or out the window!) or shutting down completely. The more we experience emotions, the greater our window of tolerance, which can adjust as life goes on. The more you do it, the bigger your window of tolerance will become. And, the bigger your window of tolerance is, the more you can deal with tough stuff in life and most importantly, your closest relationship. (Plus, you get a much more rewarding view with a wide-open window!)

So, I tried this myself. Paul and I were on an hour long drive home, which was smack in the middle of a time when I was really struggling. I was stressed at work, exhausted since I had been plagued by middle aged night sweats, and had a headache that made me feel like one of those bobbleheads that stick on a dashboard, with a head 20 times bigger than the body. I was struggling. I started to share how I was feeling. Paul, God love him, did what men do best: he tried to fix it. Yes, he did. He said, "Maybe you should try to be more positive."

"Well, why didn't I think of that?!?" I replied. "Brilliant! I will be more positive!! Yes!" I said with a very sarcastic tone.

Wrong!!

Sometimes, we need to sit in the emotions that we are feeling. Sometimes, we just need validation.

Paul responded, "Huh?"

"Honey, stop trying to fix my problems. I just want you to listen to me and validate me."

"Ok, I will just not talk?" he said. It was at this moment, he thought he had figured it out. HA, (insert eye roll).

"No Paul, that isn't what I mean. Sometimes I just need to be validated by you listening, looking at me and just saying, 'I hear you.'"

He looked at me like I had three heads. And then said, "I hear you" with an inflection upwards, as if he was still unsure.

"Well, 'A' for effort, my love. 'A' for effort!"

This is a prime example of when we can laugh at our differences with our partners. Either way, he got it and heard me. At that moment, I felt validated! I really felt safe to share my emotions with him. Which is how we create emotional connection and strength as a couple. As I mentioned earlier in the book, we are a work in progress, just like you!

DO YOU WANT IT TO WORK *OR* DO YOU WANT TO BE RIGHT?

At what cost are you willing to fight to be right? So often we can get caught up in proving a point on which we're standing firm, instead of being more focused on making it work. But ask yourself, *What is this really about? Is the topic so important that it's worth fighting over? Or is my ego getting in the way of something so frivolous that I'd be wiser to just let it go?*

Often, when we engage with our partner and fight their ego, it becomes a lose-lose prospect. I'd like to preface this though, I'm not talking about a relationship that includes any type of unsafe situations or serious mental health disorders. I'm talking about a relationship in which two people can't get along and are constantly fighting over things; constantly nitpicking, pointing out who is at fault, blaming each other, and constantly at each other's throats.

At what point will you be able to get out of your own way? What is more important to you: being right or making it work with your partner? The stronger you become, the larger your window of tolerance, the more you will want to make it work.. Now, I am not saying to default to having your partner be right all the time. But, move past the content, and be vulnerable. Share how you are feeling, and that the most important thing is being on the same team, not who's right or wrong. You will always find what you are looking for. Are you looking for your partner to be wrong or are you able to give the benefit of the doubt?

ALLOW EACH ONE TO PARENT

Allow a father to father, and a mother to mother, and stay out of the way if you want to be trusted. So often we second-guess what we're supposed to do as parents, but if we think of the relationship from a third party or a separate perspective, we know deep down that our partner has our children's best interests at heart. Obviously there are exceptions to this, but when we have children who are in homes with lots of love from both parents, we can stick to this rule, even when it's tough. We also send a message to our children when we back up our partner or go against them. Can you imagine the message that's delivered to a child when a spouse is being second guessed incessantly? Especially in front of the kids! Not only are you confusing the child, but you are being disrespectful to your partner and to yourself. You and your partner need to stick together as a team, first and foremost. Once the kiddos sneak in the middle and confuse the hierarchy, the house of cards will collapse. Don't hate me, I am just being blatantly honest here based on many, many couples I have worked with. Are you feeling provoked by this? Then perhaps you need to look in the mirror and ask yourself if your team is tightly at the top of your hierarchy.

Children learn from their parents. A child's first experience with a woman is most often with their mother and their first experience with a man is most often with their father. They watch how to interact with the opposite sex, they learn how to be a man or how to be a woman, and they will learn how to either support their spouse or show no support. The choice is up to you. You must ask yourself, *What kind of legacy do I want to leave for my children? What do I want it to look like for my grandchildren?* There's only room for one woman or one man at the top of the hierarchy. Therefore when family issues arise, or children issues arise, or any other relationship issues arise, we must keep our spouse at the top of our "hierarchy" to ensure the bond is kept and the strength of the emotional connection remains.

GROW UP!

What might you do when it comes time for you to be the rock in the relationship? You think it won't happen? Think again. Let me explain: You are at work, when you get a call that your partner has been in a horrible car accident. You are frozen in shock, and are lost for words. What will the next few months look like for you and your partner? What about your children? Have you prepared a will? Life insurance? Do you have a plan B ready to execute? I can't tell you the amount of people I come across in my counselling office who don't even know how much money their partner makes! Excuse me?!? What happened to the "till death do us part, in sickness and health, for richer and poorer—in separate bank accounts" vow? (More on this in the next chapter.)

These are the tough, often embarrassing and sometimes shameful, conversations we must have with our other halves. *But Jennifer, he shuts down when I ask him about money, or ask him about a will. It's not my fault,* you may be thinking. Believe me, I've heard it all. But my advice here is, start without them! Yes, you are already going it alone, so why wouldn't you continue to go it alone with intention, if you don't have a choice in the matter? Stop using your partner as your excuse to grow up. That's right, those magic words can be life altering. Are you ready? Let's say them together: Grow up! It's time to pull up your big girl panties, or grab your whatevers and adult. It is your responsibility to manage your finances, your plan B, your will, or any other crappy thing we need to put in place so that we aren't messed up when it happens. Take charge. You will be so empowered when you look at the document that states who will get your special Harley Davidson when you are 10 feet under (or in a vase on the fireplace since it's too bloody expensive to buy a plot these days). The legacy you live is the legacy you leave. So, are you ready for when you must adapt to a situation? Plan B is coming one way or another, like death and taxes.

Quick Tip:

Here is an example of how you could bring it up to your partner:

First off, do not approach your partner when they are knee deep in work, or watching a movie, or in a state of stress. Approach them when you are both calm and they seem ready to listen. I find car rides a great way to start, since you don't have to face your partner and they can't escape!

Honey, Marcy and Alex were telling me about this lawyer they went to to create a will. His prices were super reasonable. I didn't realize that the government would need to get involved in our business if we don't have a proper will! Geez, I hope that never happens...

In this example, you haven't once asked your partner for anything, you planted the seed. Now it's time to watch it grow. "I" statements are super powerful and help a conversation to remain focused on you and your feelings, instead of turning it into an accusatory defensive fighting match.

BE ADAPTABLE

Have you ever worked with someone who is incapable of adapting to a situation? It's tough, isn't it? Their ego gets in the way of what truly matters. Often, they stand on principle instead of trying to learn a new way to do something. Our relationships change with every new variable that may be added or taken away. It's like coaching a team of players, and then suddenly losing your best defensive player. The whole dynamic shifts. A good coach adapts, but a great coach adapts AND creates a new dynamic that's tailored to the players in front of them. Not their own ideal or how another team may set up their team. In relationships, we tend to look around instead of facing the mirror. We compare our relationship to others, compare ourselves to others, and think that what we see on Facebook or Instagram is what it's supposed to look like. Well, it doesn't and it won't. The pictures you see on social media are the best ones a person can find. Yep, we can create a facade with a few clicks of a button. Relationship propaganda is real, folks, and it's hurting countless marriages. In my experience, people who look the happiest on social media are often the saddest people in reality.

OFTEN, DIVORCE WON'T HELP

If you don't fix the way you show up in your relationships, it will continue into the next one and the next one after that. "But I can't find a partner, there are no good men left..." is what I hear so often. My response is that you will *attract* what you give. That is, you haven't attracted the person you would like to be with, yet. Start showing your authentic self, and you will attract the right person. I wonder what might happen if you drop the act and actually put yourSELF out there, not your made up self. I have a feeling you will come across people you never thought you might meet. Be vulnerable, be kind, lose the protective layer, and adapt.

GET OUT OF YOUR HEAD

Are you able to get out of your head, and into your partner's? Are you often the victim of circumstance? Well perhaps it's time to think about what's happening for others as well! Your feelings are very important, but so are your partner's. Can you find any compassion for them? Can you try to understand them and how they're feeling, even if it's hard? That's what commitment is when we marry someone, move in with someone or commit to someone. These soft compassionate moments are key for improvement.

PRIORITIES

Seek your spouse and make them your priority. Be intentional, be passionate, and laugh at their dumb jokes even if they aren't funny! Be aware and declutter your heart. Choose to be attuned to them. Join a community together. Join a club together. Do stuff together. Enjoy each other's company and build that life you want, together. No one else is going to do this for you. Be present with your partner. Don't forget to enjoy the moments. We're all so busy chasing tomorrow and planning for the future, that we induce stress instead of saying yes to the present moment. Stop, plant your feet together, go for a walk, take pictures, and just be still. Take 5 minutes off from being bitter and enjoy the moment.

THE BOTTOM LINE UNFILTERED...

In relationship therapy, we examine the cycle that exists between you and your partner. Every relationship has its own unique pattern; a dance of interactions that can either nurture or undermine the bond you share. Understanding this cycle is crucial because it shapes how you relate to one another on a daily basis. Could a daily hug honour your connection and begin to shift the dynamic? Physical touch is a powerful gesture that can communicate love and care, sometimes more effectively than words. Would seeing your relationship with loving eyes make a difference, even when you're angry or struggling to forgive? It's often said that love is a choice—a conscious decision to see the best in your partner, even during difficult times. Choosing to look at your relationship with compassion, even when you're hurt, can open the door to healing.

But what if you're finding it impossible to see through loving eyes, and a simple hug feels like too much to give? If deep hurt prevents you from feeling affection, there may be underlying issues beyond just a lack of affection or communication. These could be unhealed wounds from the past, unresolved conflicts, or unmet needs that have accumulated over time, creating emotional distance. What else has contributed to the erosion of your relationship? It's essential to identify these underlying issues, as they may be the real obstacles preventing you from reconnecting. In relationship therapy, we don't just focus on surface-level behaviours; we dig deeper to uncover the root causes of disconnection.

In the next chapter, we'll explore this cycle further and discuss steps to take if it's not working for you. We will look at how to break negative patterns and replace them with new, positive interactions that can rebuild trust and intimacy. Whether it's learning to communicate more effectively, developing empathy for each other's experiences, or finding ways to express love even when it's challenging, there are practical steps you can take to strengthen your relationship. By understanding and addressing the dynamics at play, you can begin to transform your relationship into one that is resilient, loving, and fulfilling.

Key takeaways:

1. The sooner we deal with trauma, the better.
2. Stop parenting your partner!
3. There may be some unresolved issues that require healing.

CHAPTER FOUR

Underneath it all...

*"Before you marry a person, you should first
make them use a computer with slow inter-
net connection to see who they really are."*

—WILL FERRELL—

I'm always amazed at the roles individuals play in their relationships. Some may say, "I wear the pants!" But in my marriage, the truth is, I would be lost without the strength of my husband who is "holding the pants up!" He calms me, grounds me, and loves me unconditionally. Lucky? Absolutely. But this took years of work, self discovery, and observation of one another. I might also add that we're still learning while trying to enjoy the journey along the way. At first, it wasn't pretty. We would argue, he would shut down, and I would keep talking to drive home my point; a game of cat and mouse that was extremely tiring and unproductive. I remember it almost felt like a competition. I had to be right. (And so did he!) I couldn't let it go. Little did I know that we had established a cycle that was driven by our respectively uncomfortable emotions. This makes it easy to hold grudges and to keep imaginary lists on our partners. Lists that include the times we've felt wronged. Like those annoying moments of being served the silent treatment. Newsflash: The silent treatment, holding grudges and making lists doesn't solve anything. Instead, they keep you further apart. They create an opportunity for further damage, sometimes irreversible.

In chapter two, we learned about the attachment theory and the protective behaviour of each insecure attachment style. As such, holding grudges and remembering the wrong doings of our partner makes sense if this is our protection from the hurt that was brought up in conflict. This is human nature. At face value, someone has wronged you, so why would you go back and become vulnerable, right? If a dog goes to someone, tail wagging, and that person slaps them, the dog won't forget it. They're programmed to protect themselves at all costs. While you're not that dog, your protection mode still exists, like that of an animal's. It's the protection (or what we think is protection) of shutting down, holding grudges, or remembering all the things your partner did to you that were negative that constitutes your animal-like instincts. But there are other tactics that people employ as a form of protectionism. Perhaps you're a fighter. Perhaps you raise your voice, get in your partner's face, or get bossy and try to "win."

Quick Tip:

The diagram below shows how conflict with a partner stems from avoiding the discomfort caused by underlying emotions. To break the cycle, address the emotions at the root—like pulling a dandelion by its root to prevent it from growing back.

♀ = EMOTIONS & BODY SENSATIONS (OFTEN UNCOMFORTABLE) ⇨ BEHAVIOUR ↘

→→→→→→→→→→→→→→→→→ CYCLE

♂ = EMOTIONS & BODY SENSATIONS (OFTEN UNCOMFORTABLE) ⇨ BEHAVIOUR ↗

In this chapter, not only will you understand why your cycle exists, but you will see how your unmet need (or needs) may affect your emotions and behaviour as well. The unmet needs may be the issue that has created the emotions which lead to the ways in which we behave (and attempt to protect ourselves) and explain why we enter into a cycle of conflict that replays itself over and over. In other words, it's not just the surface issue that fuels conflict, but the underlying emotions driving it. Beneath the desire to be right or the display of anger, there are often deeper emotions like fear, sadness, or hurt that can be hard to recognize or express. These hidden feelings shape how people react, and addressing them can help resolve the real source of tension. By the end of this book, you will know how to start the reconnecting journey with your partner, and will slowly be able to break down your protective mode. This is what will solve the disconnect and will foster a secure attachment style. By being open to understanding the conflict and what happens to both of you when you argue or disagree on something, you'll be better positioned to harmonize rather than be combative. Perhaps it's a co-parenting conflict, or deciding how to disperse your lottery win! Either way, challenges can become nuisances that both of you can work on, while enhancing your connection.

THE STORY OF LYNN & DAVIS

I remember a couple I worked with who almost called it quits over the debate to vaccinate or not. Lynn was vaccinated and Davis was dead set against it. Their difference of opinion created tension you could cut with a knife. It began to affect every facet of their marriage. They couldn't travel, eat out, or do much since Davis wasn't vaccinated.

I don't understand how you can sit there and allow our government to demand you to put this poison in your body!

Davis, I believe in vaccination. It has saved our population from so many other illnesses. Why can't you see that? You're such an idiot. This is one of the most idiotic decisions you've ever made!

Me?!? How can you say that?? These vaccines have not been tested yet and we won't know the outcome for years to come!

The argument was quickly building and was about to bubble over, when I simmered them down, just in time.

Lynn, what's happening for you right here, right now, at this moment? I asked.

I'm pissed! He's impossible. I really don't know how I'm going to move forward in this relationship.

Lynn, am I hearing some confusion? Frustration? Anger?

Yes, I'm angry! And I'm totally confused as to why he's being so difficult!

Let me see if I'm getting this: You're concerned that Davis is not vaccinated, worry about him getting COVID, and ultimately, very sick? Is that right?

Yes, I am worried. I am scared. We've been married for twenty-three years. This is all I know. I don't want to lose this.

I see, so is it fair to say that you generally love and care for Davis and are scared and fearful of what might happen if he isn't vaccinated? Do I have that right?

Well, yes.

Can you turn to him and tell him that?

As this exchange was occurring, the tension slowly started to come down. They were able to look at each other, be vulnerable, and speak about what was *really* going on. We were getting to the emotion that was driving their behaviour. We were getting to what was underneath it all.

I want you to imagine an umbrella. The top has many parts that all meet at one point. If you follow the seams down to the undercarriage you'll eventually find a handle. That handle represents a feeling that's guiding our behaviour. It's the device that literally holds what's presented on the outside. Lynn was experiencing true fear and worry for Davis, but initially it came out as if she was pushing her own agenda. An agenda that, at face value, can be seen as bitchy, selfish, and not very considerate of Davis' views. But if we always ask ourselves, "What is *really* going on underneath?" we can often find a reason for our behaviour.

For Lynn, it was never really about Davis not vaccinating; rather, it was about her fear of losing him. A fear so scary and uncomfortable, that our bodies will tell our brains to do anything to get away from the feeling. In this case, Lynn's anger and controlling words could easily be misunderstood for a woman who was trying to push her own agenda.

Here's a quick tip: The next time you have a significant disagreement with your partner, ask yourself, *What's really going on*? The question will often inspire you to go underneath the conflict (the umbrella, in our metaphor) and see the vulnerable reason your partner may be feeling the way they do (the handle). In essence, it's the emotion. And, so often, the emotion is one of fear. For children, behaviour is often driven by their emotions, which is an average part of development. As adults, we are supposed to teach this to our children and *demonstrate* how to regulate emotions. (Haha, that's not happening for a lot of us adults!) Many adults forget to put on their big panties, instead allowing their emotions to guide their behaviour, which is more of a child-like approach rather than a measured adult approach. In other words, they're allowing their emotions to get the better of them. When this happens, our behaviour often masks what we're really feeling. And if what we're feeling hurts us, then you can appreciate how one's behaviour is used to protect us from examining our true emotions.

Emotions are like dashboard lights, signalling what's happening inside. Some are urgent warnings, like running out of fuel, while others simply indicate your current state, like your speed. Either way, they are indicators of what's going inside your body. When we ignore them (or are unaware of them), we can do damage externally. Just like a car, if you ignore all the warning signs, your car will not last long. Take the time to look underneath the hood. Take the time to see it all and know how it works. You'll thank me later!

As I've mentioned previously, I see showing emotion as a strength. Ask yourself, *Is it easier to shut down and act the role of bitch, or to share that you are really scared of what might happen? Would short term pain give me long term gain?* The truth is, the battle is often found in the silence. In the case of Lynn and Davis, had Lynn shared from the beginning that she was uber scared and fearful of losing him, she may have been met with an empathetic response and the tension might never have occurred. Oftentimes it's useful to let our hearts speak before we let the mind do the talking. Had Lynn shown her heart instead of her head (behaviour/thoughts/opinions), their interactions would likely have been much more loving. And, most importantly, they would have kept their emotional connection intact. We must protect the emotional connection at all costs.

Could you imagine a world in which we did protect our connections? A world where we didn't allow our egos to get in the way? Specifically, I'm talking about the ego part of ourselves that's afraid of being judged, seen as wrong, irrational, lost...anything unfavourable, and will always do what it can to avoid that, including bulldozing over others' wants and needs in the process. In the end, Davis needed Lynn's heart, not her mind. That is, he needed the vulnerable feelings to come through instead of the opinions that came out of those emotions. If we choose to respect our partners' decisions in life, i.e., vaccinations, in Lynn and Davis' case, our relationships will foster a respectful, equitable bond that can sustain the strongest of storms. Ask yourself, *At what cost do I need to be right?* In the end, do you want to be right, or do you want your relationship to work? You choose!

When a couple gets into a positive rhythm or balance, the process can be incredibly rewarding and nurturing for a family. But when the rhythm is one of dissonance, havoc can ensue. No rhythm and no team equals no peace. When there's a lack of harmony, we can easily settle into bad habits with our partners and can get sucked into a cycle that can escalate the conflicts that keep us stuck in our relationships. These habits form over time and often trigger in a matter of mere seconds. This is why so many people have a hard time in relationships.

For example, when we were first married and Paul would get angry, I would engage and try to fix whatever he was angry about. Then he would get more angry. I would get emotional and start making it about him. Then, all of a sudden, I was the problem instead of the problem being the problem. We went from him feeling a very valid emotion (anger) to being frustrated with his wife who was in his space. At that moment, he was probably thinking, *Man, she is so annoying. Why can't she stay out of my business and just let me be? Ugh, life would be so easy without her.* Meanwhile, I was thinking: *What is his problem? I am only trying to help! How could he be so mean to me! Poor me; this marriage stinks.* Does any of this sound familiar to you? Anger itself isn't inherently negative; it's a natural human emotion that often signals a deeper issue, such as frustration, hurt, or injustice. When anger leads to destructive behaviors like hitting, screaming, or losing control, the emotion is being expressed in unhealthy and damaging ways. These actions not only harm others but also perpetuate a cycle of unresolved emotions. However, anger can be channelled constructively, used as a tool for reflection and positive change. It's possible to feel anger without resorting to harmful actions, by addressing the root cause and expressing it calmly and respectfully. Recognizing this distinction allows for healthier emotional regulation and better outcomes in personal and social interactions.

If we look at these emotions as the top layer of the root of our challenges, then we realize there must be something much deeper. For instance, anger is often a cover-up for fear. I have even heard some therapists claim that anger isn't a true emotion. It's much easier to be an angry man than one who's fearful of not being good enough, being "a screw up," or failing at being a husband. In other words, the emotions underneath drive the behaviour, which is just a symptom. So ask yourself next time, what's really going on underneath the anger?

Amongst the men I've worked with in couples therapy, I've discovered a pattern that's fairly universal: Men often fashion a response to their wives that represents a protection of the vulnerable emotion they so desperately want to hide. This is what's lying beneath the surface. Like a lion fighting and protecting itself, it will fight its prey to the bitter end, rather than risk being hurt itself. The fight (or the behaviour) is the symptom of what's really happening. It's a no-win situation—and a dangerous one as well. However, let's not single out men here. Women, just as often, play the role of the imperilled and desperate lioness by masking the emotions they're too afraid to examine. As you can imagine, these types of lion fights are unsafe. At this point, the lion's den is off limits. The other partner will shut down and stay outside the cage. It is scary to enter the den, when the lion is angry.

As mentioned in Chapter two, we learn how to protect ourselves based on what happened to us as children. Adverse Childhood Experiences (ACE) and childhood trauma are the wounds/memories that prompt us to put up walls and add a protective layer that we believe is required for safety. This is our warning system that is intrinsic to who we are as mammals. It's a good thing when needed; it protects us. But unfortunately, it continues into adulthood and will show up anytime the alarm is triggered, even when there is no emergency. So, now it may be constricting you from connecting with your loved one. And your body may believe it's still in danger—even when it's not. Your body is doing its job even though whatever protective mechanism you employ isn't needed or required any longer. You see, it's a response. Now, your body needs to be taught it's safe so that you can be emotionally connected to your partner.

Getting back to our lion metaphor, it's not a good time to jump into the lion's den when the animal's teeth are ready to eat its prey. You know yourself well. Would anyone be able to get close to you when you're in a state of protection, with teeth exposed? Perhaps it's time to work with a therapist so that your body can learn to release an archaic defence mechanism. Once that happens, you'll be able to reap the benefits of being in a loving, safe relationship, no longer triggered by experiences of your past (or at the very least, understanding your triggers).

Maybe you grew up in a loving, safe home. It's possible that you're emotionally accessible to your partner. If you are, you're one of the lucky ones! However, the cycle that exists between both of you can still create major conflict. You may still have traumas in your life that have stuck with you and have left scars. But whether you have a secure attachment style or an insecure one, it's useful to understand our patterns and cycles when we engage with our partners and to look under the surface to share our emotions and to become aware of them. I've seen couples shift from being in total protection mode, to tiptoeing into the lion's den, to totally petting the lion. It's such an incredible transformation to witness, but one that only happens if members are willing to open themselves to being vulnerable and "show-up" with their partner. Vulnerability is probably the scariest concept for most, especially if they're coming from a traumatic background or adverse experiences having peppered their lives. Nevertheless, the results can be transformative.

THE BOTTOM LINE UNFILTERED...

A traumatic background or experiencing adversity can teach us how to be in a relationship from a very young age. We learn who we count on and who we can trust. In my practice,

I have been shocked, time and time again, at the number of people who have been sexually and emotionally violated in some capacity. These violations influence how we show up later in our lives, and can create obstacles that will take work and vulnerability to overcome. Understanding how our past experiences show up today, however, can enhance our treatment and assist in our attempts at repairing our relationships.

This does not mean you are totally doomed if you have had bad stuff happen. It means that you have some work to do and may require a good therapist who may help you. And as mentioned earlier, ironically, divorce won't help. The pattern is almost certain to repeat itself in the next relationship. For example, as parents, it's tempting to protect our children from situations by fixing or taking them right out of the situation. I see many kids moving schools halfway through the year; their parents believing that a fresh start will fix the issues. Six months later, the issues have magically appeared at the new school. It's not what we do for our kids, but what we teach them to do for themselves that makes all the difference. To work through the conflict is key. To learn about ourselves in that moment, and to feel the discomfort, is what will help you in your next relationship. If you can do all this with your partner, and you still both decide to go your separate ways, then you have had the opportunity to learn about your patterns, triggers, and what you really want in a relationship. As well, it may improve your ability to co-parent in a calm way, and may improve a transition out of the relationship. Remember, you are your patterns, and they will follow you wherever you go until you fix them.

Your pattern that gets established amongst you and your partner, is keeping you stuck. You know the pattern I am talking about? The one where you get angry, complain and talk at them, then they shut down, walk away; and as a result, you both feel like crap. You are left with "what the hell just happened? I am the one who was wronged here!" and your partner may feel like you are being a total jerk. Or perhaps you are the one who shuts down to avoid the conflict. It probably feels better to shut down than to face the conflict head on. Unfortunately, damage is done with every conflict that's not worked out. The cycle makes sense though, if you break it down. If you continually talk and get escalated when trying to get your point across, this may be a strategy that you've devised (probably unknowingly) that aims to tame your anxiety or the bad feeling in the pit of your stomach. *If only I could make them understand how I feel, then I will feel better.* Instead, you are *telling* them what you think, not what you feel. Make sense? And for your partner who is the avoider, they may be thinking, *what's the point? I can't do anything right. I'm such a failure.* The cycle that exists between the two of you will continue until you fix it! It's like a monster eating away at the relationship that exists between the two of you. Let's tell that monster to get lost!

Applying that principle to ourselves, if we leave our partners without trying to fix how we show up in our relationships, then we are surely leaving room for our patterns to resurface in our next relationship. I'm not saying that divorce is out of the question; rather, it's a smart move to communicate and try to get in touch with who we are in a relationship before calling it quits. Neither you or your partner is a monster. But the patterns that exist between the two of you represent the creature that lurks in the shadowy depths, beneath the surface of your relationship. It's the habit, the programming, and how you show up in relationships. Have you ever wondered why you have no luck finding a partner? Or why you continually choose the wrong person? Well, often they fit the pattern that you have created along the way.

So, are you ready to get rid of your monster? Ready to disrupt the cycle/pattern that exists between you and your partner? Ready to fight the monster? Are you ready to figure out what's underneath it all and allow the underlying emotions to speak instead of allowing your brain to do the talking, which may lead you into a protective mode? It has to start with you. Even if your partner's unaware of what you're learning right now, I can tell you that there's power in revealing your emotions. And in doing so, you will likely create the space, and an example to follow, for your partner to follow suit.

My Bold & Brave Diary...

Think about the last time you and your partner had a conflict. In a nutshell, what was it about? What was the conflict? What was the trigger?

T—

_____

_____

_____

_____

_____

Now, what were you feeling when you were triggered? Try to go deeper than anger...were you hurt? Embarrassed? Devastated? If it helps, refer to the back of the book for a list of emotions.

E—

_____

_____

_____

_____

_____

What was your little tiny voice telling you in your head, about YOU? Not your partner, but about you!! What is your negative narrative? Not good enough? Are you needy? (Insert growl-) You are a failure? What is your negative narrative telling you? Remember, this is only your belief ... but it is important to be honest with yourself. If you are struggling to figure it out, think about your childhood and what your negative belief about yourself was.

M—

_____

_____

_____

How do you respond in the moment? Do you lash out? Do you shut down for a few days? Or maybe you leave the room? This is where the protection of your emotions comes in. Your protections from the feeling you have when your negative narrative is exposed. At all costs, our internal system will fight to keep our vulnerabilities secret and safe. So, how do you behave in the moment? What is your protection mechanism?

P—

_____

_____

_____

So, when you enter into conflict, remember to lower your TEMP! 9 times out of 10, your temper will land you in hot water!

Key takeaways:

1. Children act on emotions, adults make a plan and follow through.
2. Your patterns are keeping you stuck.
3. It's not what we do for our kids, but what we teach them to do for themselves that makes all the difference.

CHAPTER FIVE

Show Me the Money

"Money often costs too much!"
—RALPH WALDO EMERSON—

Why is it that we'll make babies with our partners, but we won't pay for a portion of the electrical bill? Or we'll take 50% of the restaurant tab, *unless it's a birthday of course,* then we'll foot the entire bill as a special treat! [Insert eye roll.] Hmm. I wonder how the bill would be split if you had two *extra* breadsticks at the *Olive Garden*, but only ordered a side salad? (Please, for the love of Pete, bring back the *Olive Garden* to Canada!!)

Does this sound reasonable to you? Money continues to be a taboo topic amongst many couples (and therapists); but since I want to give you the best possible advice, I think it's a vital topic, and deserves an entire chapter!

Money doesn't bring out the evil in us. Instead, money often brings out our true colours, which will include our negative tendencies, including greed, hoarding, spending mindlessly or even hiding purchases, if that's part of who we are. In fact, many people think that the Bible says that money is the root of all evil. But that wouldn't be accurate. The Bible actually says that the *love of money* is the root of all evil. So, your propensity to delve into the world of evil is contingent upon what you love and what you value. But money itself isn't bad. It may, as a matter of fact, provide you the means to do a lot of good deeds. Money can bring out generosity, and a giving nature too, if that's a part of your makeup. So, the question is: Where do you fit in on this spectrum? What do you value most of all? Your marriage or your money? If you said "my money," then I have no wise words for you, except that you may want to find a damn good therapist and a cheap lawyer. If you said, "my marriage," then here are some suggestions on how to approach your finances in peace and in love.

First off, stop being a baby! Yes, I just called you childish; but you may have needed to hear this! Why else would you compare what he bought for himself to what you didn't buy for yourself? *It's not fair!* Well, if you haven't figured that one out yet, you might be replaying a scene right out of your elementary school lunch hour. Life is not about being fair and neither are relationships. Remember in Chapter 4, we learned the 80/20 rule? It's the rule that allows you to create an infinite amount of combinations to make 100%. Think about how that strategy could be useful here. Consider how an equitable approach to sharing may be healthier than assuming every bill needs to be split equally. If you think your relationship should be fair, you will be disappointed. I can't think of many couples who have a loving, emotionally close relationship that'll last forever while *not* sharing details about finances, and putting the money above the relationship. I'm not talking about those couples who've been married for 50+ years and hate each other, but share money. That's not loving, and maybe a shotgun wedding gone wrong.

Finances are a crucial part of relationships, something that often splits couples apart. But usually, finances are a symptom of something larger. Often, the relationship is lacking love and understanding, or most importantly, trust, whenever there are money issues. A loving, understanding, trusting relationship has TLC...tender, loving, care (not tender, loving, *cash*). However, not being able to share money or talk about money, could stem from other places besides the current relationship. Financial trauma from other parts of your life could be hindering you.

Is it loving to ask your partner to pay a bill? Is it caring to have your partner pick up the children, because it's their turn (even though they just finished a twelve hour shift and you have a day off)? What about having your daughter's pet snake's cage cleaned out? Maybe it's your partner's turn, but maybe they're petrified of snakes. How do you view these scenarios? I often encounter these types of scenarios from couples who pride themselves on being fair. These are normally the couples who keep score, and make it known when they've done more than their partner. "You didn't pay me back for the groceries! Can you etransfer me?" Hmm, isn't that odd? Is the money not yours if you got divorced or your partner were to pass away? So, why not make it easy on yourself now and just start sharing in the responsibilities?

Now, examine these scenarios using a lens with a little TLC. How about paying the bill from a joint account? Not fair, but loving! YOU pick up your child instead of your exhausted partner. Not fair, but very caring! You offer to clean the snake pit out again. Again, very tender and loving and caring! But sooo not fair! If you're already doing some of these things in this way in your relationship, then why don't you do it with money? It's no different than cleaning the snake pit! Or is it?

What is money to you? Is it power? Is it safety? Control? You can have all those things with your partner too. Is money evil in itself? No. But our desire for it often costs us more than we think. And its negative effects on our lives, when we do obtain it, are often understated and overlooked. Especially when it never returns the personal benefits we think it will. Remember: You can never have enough of what won't satisfy you. Therefore, keeping money in its proper place in our affections is a daily and lifelong struggle for many. So, hear me out: Stop being a baby, take off the bib,, and open a damn joint account where both your pay cheques go! You may be cursing at me now, but before you make any decisions on how you feel about this advice, keep reading. After all, you bought this book so you could find out what your therapist really wants to tell you about relationships, and ultimately, what works!

I've had lots of success and failures working with couples when feelings need to be brought to the forefront, or if an apology is required; buuuuuuut, whenever I bring up finances, I often get a death stare. It's as if the couple morph into Nurse Ratched and Lord Voldemort; with their laser piercing eyes burning a hole into the little soft spot in-between my clavicles; just so that I can stop talking.

MONEY.

It's a scary word for many that's both a source of shame *and* power.

MONEY.

These five little letters can bring a relationship into the depths of despair and divorce.

MONEY.

We can't live without it. But wait; perhaps MONEY is not the problem.

When working with couples, I often dig deep into the core issues that have brought them into my office. Ironically, I've never had a couple write in their intake form, "Money issues." So why is it that when the subject is brought up, it often causes people to stop in their tracks and avoid it at all costs (pardon the pun!)? In my time as a therapist, I've heard many stories of struggles and adversities related to money. Generally, it's because there isn't enough of it. But what about an abundance of money? Could that also cause problems in a relationship? And what might money represent to couples?

THE STORY OF ROSS...

One such client, Ross, a top-notch sales guru, had the gift of the gab. He'd been successful in talking his way to the top. He came to our first session dressed in an expensive suit and shiny shoes. He looked the part of the stereotypical rich dude from the *dude-culture* corporate world. But it quickly became clear that this wasn't the case at all. Well, not anymore at least. He came to me after he'd lost $179,260 at a high stakes poker match after he'd travelled to Las Vegas with some colleagues (that number is etched in my memory from the countless times it was said in session). All of his colleagues witnessed the substantial loss. But Ross played it off like it was a drop in the bucket through his confident laugh and pearly white smile. Little did they know, it would end him in more ways than one.

Once his wife found out what had happened, she left him. She said he needed help before she would consider the prospect of working it out. Ross, however, had a history of spending, gambling, and using money to try to win over colleagues, to impress others, and to feel powerful. He did this behind his wife's back, which had been an ongoing problem. When she finally found out the magnitude of his unfaithfulness with his mistress (the money), she bailed. Then, he hit rock bottom.

If the misuse and spending of money was the symptom, what could have been the main problem? What had been driving his behaviour? Remember from Chapter 2, behaviour in a relationship is a reflection of what's going on inside of us, based on what's happened.

So, what happened to Ross?

When we started to explore some of his life's struggles, Ross was able to share easily, without many prompts. I was quite surprised that he could so readily talk about his challenges. Ross was a good talker, and successful; so much so that he could sell sawdust to a lumber mill! His go-to was to use his charm and charisma to avoid any uncomfortable feelings or conflict. I slowly realized he was talking his way out of my office as well. I was being fooled like the lumber mill; and then, I called *bull*. And bull it was...

It took a lot of "gentle nudging" before I had the gall to push him, which was needed in his case. Ross had great difficulty accessing his emotions and the effects the emotions were having on his body. He had spent over fourty years avoiding being uncomfortable in both his body and his thoughts, and had created a great protection against it –talking. So, this in itself, was going to be a little mountain to climb together. Remember in chapter two, certain attachment styles can lead one to form a protective shell around one's emotions. Examples are lashing outward or inward, substance abuse, shutting down, pursuing an argument, and other such protection mechanisms. Our protective shell can pop up in a split second, to protect ourselves from the uncomfortable feelings that come when we face the hard stuff.

What is your protection? How do you respond when you are provoked?

After a few sessions, I introduced EMDR therapy to Ross. EMDR stands for Eye Movement Desensitization and Reprocessing and is not "talk therapy." Rather, it's a somatic therapy that accesses emotions through the body instead of through conversation. A client is led by the therapist, to move their eyes back and forth, across their visual field, in various ways. Extensive research shows this method of therapy is widely recognized and highly beneficial when working with emotions. (If you are interested in this form of therapy, check out EMDRIA for more detail.)

Have you ever had an aroma that reminds you of a pleasant memory? Or perhaps a negative memory? This is the essence of somatic therapy. For example, when I see or smell guacamole or *Irish Spring*, I get nauseous. When I was pregnant and had horrible morning sickness, my husband was using *Irish Spring* soap every morning, and we had guacamole in the fridge. So, my body, to this day, associates the smell and sight of those things with sickness. Make sense? Or perhaps you got drunk off Bacardi Red and were riding the porcelain bus when you were a teenager. Ugh... I still can't look at that stuff when I'm in the liquor store.

Ross, however, could persuade a dog to give him its only bone, with his charisma and skill; to the point that he believed his own bulls**t. But with EMDR, we use the body's disturbance that comes up when triggered, to trace back to the commencement of a possible trauma. We use the body to guide the healing, instead of our thoughts. So, when I brought up the experience of him losing the $179,260 chunk of money, I asked him what he felt in his body.

Umm, nothing...

Really? Ok, then it doesn't bother you that you lost it?

Well, of course it does. But I don't feel it.

Ok, then, tell me why it bothers you.

Well, obviously...(rolling his eyes)

Obviously what?

Obviously I lost a huge part of my investments, and then my wife left me.

Your investments? Then why was she so mad if it belonged to you?

Well, it's for both of us. I guess it's our investments. But I'm the one who made the money to put into those investments!

Has this been a conflict between you two? Mine and ours?

Sometimes.

Ok, nooowww do you feel anything?

No.

I see your eyes are wet.

His chin quivered and then he snorted and said, "Nothing." Then proceeded to sob.

I stopped for a few minutes, then asked him about how money was handled in the household.

Ross eventually shared that he had had a tough time letting anyone know about his personal finances, even his wife. This had been a cause of tension in their home. She felt like she didn't matter and wasn't enough for him; feeling that, otherwise, he would trust her with the money. But Ross told me this was not about trusting his wife. He said he trusted her wholeheartedly. It was something else, but he couldn't put his finger on it. We continued to explore...

Do you have any fears?

None.

Maybe not spiders or mice, but what about being broke and starving?

His eyes opened wide. There it was, one single word: STARVING.

I saw the changed charismatic expression and knew there was a disturbance. I started there, enabling him to access the emotions in his body that were creating a dissonance within him. Eventually, he was able to pinpoint the uncomfortable sensations.

We all feel disturbances differently, and they can appear anywhere in the body. For Ross, it was in his chest, hands, and face. Where might you feel a disturbance when you think about how you and your partner handle money?

Quick Tip:

Take a moment to reflect on what you've just read. Bring up the last conflict you and your partner had about money. How disturbing did it feel in your body from 0-10 (0 would be no disturbance, and 10 is the worst disturbance you can imagine)? Where do you feel it? Notice it, now cross your arms over your chest so that your hands are lying comfortably on your chest like an "X." Now, tap each hand, one at a time, and continue to alternate taps. This is called bilateral tapping, also known as the butterfly hug. Continue to tap until you can feel your number go down on the scale of 0-10.

Ross and I did a "floatback," which is a technique used to access a flood of memories, including the earliest memory Ross could recall of being cold and starving. He was four years old, in an apartment with his mother and brother. When his mother wasn't looking, his brother took his piece of potato. The memories began flooding-in. Ross remembered the piece of potato and the wallpaper in the apartment that was orange, which he used to pretend was a warm fire. But he remembered that the room was always cold and drafty. As he brought-up that memory, he began to cry.

We continued with bilateral eye movements, which is how EMDR processes the disturbance of the memory. The goal in EMDR is to continue the bilateral eye movements and continue feeling the emotions. The combination of eye movements and the feeling of emotion facilitates "processing." Think of a piece of paper crumpled up and jammed into a drawer. Now, imagine taking it out, smoothing out the paper, and putting it in a file folder, tucked away in a drawer. That's what reprocessing is like. One activates a memory, feels the emotions that come up, then proceeds to notice the feelings. Often, we block emotions that are difficult to feel. Laughing, talking, shifting body language, can all be ways to block emotions that may be coming out. But with EMDR, we are trying to notice the uncomfortable emotions, so they can "get out" and stay out! At this stage, we're desensitizing the memory in terms of how it's categorized. This includes the negative thoughts about yourself (afterall, Ross was just a child, it wasn't his fault that he was starving), and then reprocessing them by categorizing with positive thoughts about oneself. In simple terms, moving from "I am not good enough" to "I am good enough" or by employing a similar statement.

Usually by this point, the client realizes that they're human and not responsible for how they came to develop this reaction. This is how trauma rewires the brain. The crumpled up paper is the trauma. When we have an adverse childhood experience, our brains naturally add a negative thought about ourselves; especially as children. Children are egocentric (which is what they're supposed to be). This thought usually involves safety, responsibility, or choice. Once we can let ourselves off the hook, and move past the trauma by associating the memory with a positive thought about ourselves, the disturbance will go away. It's like developing a filing cabinet full of flattened papers. Sure, they may have many creases, but now they're organized and take up less space. They're also easier to scrutinize and understand.

If you are thinking, *Yeah right; move my eyes and I'll feel better*, there's much more to it; but yes, it seems hokey! Well, I was skeptic *numero uno* with regard to this therapy. Remember in my prologue I mentioned my husband, Paul, had a fall and broke his neck? I had flashbacks of the incident for years. I heard about EMDR and thought it was completely "hippy-dippy." But I tried it anyway, because I was desperate for a decent night's sleep without seeing Paul's accident careen across my mind. I had a few sessions of EMDR, bawled my eyes out, and never had another flashback again. I can talk about the accident, and it doesn't make me want to puke anymore. Of course it's still a sad story, but my body no longer responds in a fight or flight way when I think about it. That state of fight or flight is precisely the consequence of unresolved trauma. Our minds may know we're safe, but our bodies continue to think we're in danger. This is because our bodies are stuck in the experience. So EMDR can take away the body's disturbance, which often drives our behaviour. As mentioned above, gambling was not the problem; rather, it was a symptom. The problem was being driven by the trauma response. The gambling was the protection to the trauma response. So, if we heal the trauma, the symptom of gambling (protection) will go away. It doesn't necessarily remove the associated emotion, but it's a fabulous resolve with regard to the body's reaction. For example, a death may be sad before and after EMDR, but it may no longer give you terrible stomach pains or shortness of breath. Spiders will forever be scary to me, but I don't panic and hyperventilate anymore when I see one; all thanks to the EMDR work I've done around this phobia.

Ross processed his unresolved trauma and was able to move on. He connected his memory of being a cold, starving child to his desire for money, as a means of never starving again. The "thrill" he spoke of was also traced back to him wanting to take control of his situation; a desire that transformed into a need for power. It was all a facade, and he never realized it. He was then able to remember that, as a child, his brother often took things away from him, including attention from his mother. Ross recalled feeling like a shadow; nothing was ever good enough and he was always compared to his brother.

We spent months talking about many of the memories that came up in EMDR, and then continued with some more targets (a term used in EMDR to describe the event/person/ idea that brings up the body disturbance). After our work had come to an end, Ross reported that he no longer felt the desire to gamble. I remember him saying, "The strangest thing happened: I went to the casino, sat down at a table, and just watched. I didn't have any desire to play!" The symptom of something much bigger went away, once the "much bigger something" was explored. Eventually, Ross and his wife got back together and worked with a therapist to improve their communication. She too, had some unresolved trauma that had to be cleared.

My Bold & Brave Diary...

How might the above anecdote apply to you and your partner? Is there unresolved trauma in your life? Perhaps a past affair or breakup? Or a present worry about your own safety and money? It may be time to seek help so that you, too, can be free from the symptoms that are causing stress in your relationship.

Take a moment to reflect on these questions. If you could erase any event from your life, which one would it be? Why?

_____

_____

_____

_____

_____

THE BOTTOM LINE UNFILTERED

When we have open communication and discussions about money with our respective partners, we become closer and have opportunities to build trust in a way that's deeply profound. Often, one partner may earn far more than the other but it certainly doesn't mean that one person is worth more than the other. It's utter bull to believe that a fifty percent contribution to the finances is equal to a balanced relationship. Think about it, what happens when a person gets hurt or sick? Does their worth decrease because their taxable income does too? Imagine you had a horrible accident, falling onto your pet raccoon, sailing forward, knocking yourself out, along with your incisors; all thanks to a banana peel. Your face modeling gig is kaput and your vet bill is astronomical. *Oy Vey!* Now what? You might not feel so worthy anymore; perhaps because you have a pet raccoon and never really meant that the entirety of the relationship was 50/50. This happens with a lot of people who are the "breadwinners" in the family: they say it, but they don't mean it.

How is a couple supposed to plan for their future and attain their financial goals if they don't discuss what their fixed and variable costs are? Finances have become the number one reason people split up. This isn't to say that we shouldn't be working hard to provide for our families—certainly that *is* the case. Nor does it mean that we should turn down honest compensation. But, too often, our desire to accumulate money stands in the way of seeing things clearly. What matters most, however, is what's between the money and your partner. It's the relationship; the third entity (more on this in the next chapter); the thing that YOU need to honour, even when the going gets tough. Yes, even when it comes to money; especially when it never returns the personal benefits we think it will. But by contrast, when you focus on the relationship, you're focusing on a lifelong partner who has your back, no matter what. It's precisely that emotional connection through the relationship that'll allow you to trust one another when it comes to the cash. And believe me, it'll be far easier to create wealth when you're both aligned.

Here's a simple question: What do you value most in life? If you answered "my partner," then why are you putting money ahead of them? Keeping money in its proper place in our affections is a daily and lifelong struggle. You can never have enough of something that just can't satisfy you. Let me say this again: You can NEVER have enough of something that will NEVER satisfy you! You will NEVER have enough money. You will NEVER be satisfied. You may be saying, "Not true, Jennifer. If I had that Porsche 911 and the new iPhone 74, I would be very happy!" But what happens when the iPhone 75 and 76 come out and they include a live-in personal assistant? You'll likely up the ante because you imagine the little personal assistant dusting your collection of fuzzy dice from the 1970s would make you happier. Face it: You'll never stop trying to earn the buck, until you get in touch with the fact that the biggest problem was never the money to begin with.

The money was never the problem.

The money was never the problem.

Remember in chapter two, I explained the attachment theory and how it applies to you? If you look back at those teachings, remember what happens to us and how we show up in a relationship, if we have anything but a secure attachment style. In the absence of a secure attachment style, a void will be felt. That empty space will be present until we uncover what happened to you in your life to lead you to a place where you are untrusting or feeling unsafe in your relationship. This is not meant to be literal safety; it's an emotional safety. (If there is ever a threat of physical, mental, or emotional safety, this chapter is not meant for you... please seek help!) Emotional safety, when attained, will begin to fill the void that's present. It will be as if you are always connected to your partner, even if you are not physically together. But when there's a void, you can be lonely in a room of thousands of people. So alone, so desperately alone, that money can be your friend in the moment. This will be short lived though, once your visa is maxed and declined. Your house of cards will collapse, like a drunken sailor on payday! Or, you might resort to alcohol. Yes, that can be a void filler too! Buuuutt you may do damage to your liver, life, and relationships. Or, how about some porn? It's the quickest growing addiction in North America. You get the picture: The money, and all the other "void fillers" are not the root cause of the behaviour behind it. So, how do you get rid of a weed? You get the root.

What's stopping YOU from talking about and sharing your finances, including the struggles and successes? Is it shame? Fear? Perhaps you've had a terrible experience in the past. Or perhaps your partner's a gambling addict or is addicted to travelling to Kevin Baconfests around the world. This goes back to the idea that money paradigms are a symptom of something bigger. So, what is the "much bigger?" No one gambles away their life savings for kicks...or admits they follow Kevin Bacon!

How committed are you to this relationship? Can you share money or just the kids? Perhaps you want to start sharing money, and are wondering how. Here are a few ways you can learn how to start building safety, strength, and stability with your finances and your partner:

FINANCIAL TIP #1: TALK ABOUT FINANCES BY TAKING A SIMPLE FINANCIAL COURSE:

Your next step is to think about finances and what it would take to talk about your own finances with your partner. If you're not there yet, could you talk about finances in general? Take an online course in financial literacy, together, to get the ball rolling. YNAB is a Canadian Budget App that has lessons and a YouTube channel with instructions on how to achieve financial peace. Try it! Or find another guide, but get something that is a simple course that explains the importance of planning, how to invest, how to save for your future, how to budget, and the most important part: how to do it together. Then, move on to your own finances once you are on the same page about finances in general.

FINANCIAL TIP #2: OPEN A JOINT ACCOUNT:

As I mentioned in the beginning of this chapter, open a joint bank account, even if you aren't ready to use it. By opening a joint account, you not only have to figure out where you want to bank together, but you will need to make an appointment, talk about what type of account you'll need, and will be faced with a personal money conversation. This tiny step can shake things up a bit. It can also get you on the road to trusting your partner (and yourself) with money. Perhaps a monthly meeting is scheduled over dinner. I know these things don't always happen, but if you plan it with intention (and put it in your iphone 75), then it may get done!

FINANCIAL TIP #3: 80/20 RULE:

Remember in previous chapters, the idea of making things equal 100% together, as a team? Well, it can apply here too! "Our relationship is 50/50. It works for us. She pays the hydro and I pay the water bill." But what happens when you throw in the accident you have when skydiving with your pet raccoon. Not only did you break your leg, but your beloved BooBooBear sauteed you like an onion on the swift decline. You are now a BooBoo yourself! The bills will pile up while on sick leave. Will it continue to work at 50/50? How will it feel if you're the partner who's stuck in bed recovering, knowing your partner is working two jobs to make ends meet? Or perhaps you're the one working two jobs, and are resentful of your partner for being so stupid to dive out of a plane with a company that just opened with a business named, *Dive or Die.* You probably wouldn't feel great during this hardship. Perhaps your true hardship may look different than this scenario; but ultimately, when the hardships happen, we are usually not ready.

I will never forget the devastation of knowing my husband could no longer run his carpentry business. We were on our way to a life of financial security, or so we thought. We were young twenty-something year olds, invincible, living it up, without a care in the world. We didn't think about critical illness insurance, or any other type of security measure. We were on cloud nine, about to be married and embark on a life together: careers, a new home, and nothing stopping us. Until that fateful day. One fall. That's all it took. One moment in time that I've replayed over and over again in my mind.

I can still see Paul falling, and my arm extended, trying desperately to catch him, his head bouncing off the concrete, blood everywhere. Come to think of it, I collected his teeth for some strange reason, and put them somewhere safe. If you find the missing ones, please let me know! I never did!!

That one moment in time changed the trajectory of our entire life. I have worked two jobs for twenty years to make ends meet and to provide for our family. I am known as the breadwinner, sugarmama, main income earner, provider, meal ticket, and I hate it. I hate being known as this. And it's not the job of a man to do this. Nor is it a 50/50 agreement. This is what works for me and Paul. As I mentioned early on in the book, he is my rock and I would be lost without him. There is no amount of money that can ever replace a man who strives to be a better man every day and a partner who honours his wife. I wouldn't change him for the world; he is already my world.

Unfortunately though, what we've gone through hasn't been easy for him, as a man. I have heard a few comments from other men he hangs out with that are low blows and, quite frankly, heartless. I will truly never understand the culture of male companionship, which includes busting each other's balls for fun. No, thanks!

So, through this experience, I learned how important it is to look at relationships from an equitable viewpoint instead of an equal one. Equitable means to divvy up based on need and abilities. Equality means that everyone gets the same, no matter the privilege or ability. So, think about it: Doesn't it make more sense to run your life in an equitable way? You just might be in a position, one day, where you will only be able to cover 20% and will need to lean on your partner for the 80%. So, instead of the 50/50 concept that has ruined countless relationships, I want you to think for a moment of how many ways you can make up 100 by adding two numbers. Infinite ways (when you include decimals), right? Now think about when you got food poisoning because you ate bad sushi when there was a 50% off sale. You missed a full week of work. Imagine you are no longer 50/50, but know together you make 100%. While trying to forget the greyish coloured california roll you devoured, you are only a small 17%. You are too sick to make up your 50%. Your partner understands because you have already adopted the mindset of the 80/20 rule. You need your partner to be the remaining 83%, and they do it with love and understanding. Together, you make up 100%, all of the time! You will never be short. And you know your partner will have your back, and the puke bucket! Now imagine the reverse. There will come a time when you will need to be the 83% or whatever percentage is required. Life is unpredictable and you can't bank on anything. But if you have a team that you can rely on (your partner), then you know you'll be okay. You can apply this to all areas of your relationship. When your mother passed away (God rest her soul), you weren't at your best. You needed space to grieve. Your partner picked up the slack. If you are thinking, "no they didn't," then this rule is made for you!

FINANCIAL TIP #4: NO MORE LISTS:

Do you know *the list*? It's the list that pops up when you're really angry with your partner. It's the imaginary list in your mind that continually keeps the negative score of your partner, without them knowing it. The list that drives your behaviour when he asks you to pass the salt and you pounce on him like a pissed off cat. The list that you may be used to having so you have some ammo to rely on when you both argue about money. This list is fueling the fire, and is not helpful. As things come up, and we learn to deal with them, the list becomes unnecessary.

Get rid of your list by communicating! Talk to your partner; tell them you're mad they bought Enron shares instead of Apple shares back in 1999. Tell them you were angry when they bought you monster sized club speakers off the back of a truck in the Home Depot parking lot, instead of the necklace you would have liked (true story! My basement is rockin' like a 90s club). Then, show them the list you made about all the good things you love about them and why you were attracted in the first place. What would you tell your daughter (even if you don't have one) if she was going through a hard time with her spouse? Trust is built with time and believable behaviour that's demonstrated through action, and meaningful moments. But first you must get out of your own way, because we can be our own worst enemies sometimes.

You must be wondering what happened to Ross. Well, once
he came to terms with the cause of his gambling addiction,
he asked his wife to join him in therapy. They went through
some rough waters together and talked about really hard
stuff. One activity that I had them do was to create a list of
non-negotiables, individually. This is not just around finances,
it's all encompassing. If you're thinking, a red shiny corvette
by the age of 50, you're not on the right track. These non-
negotiables are what help you stay true to who you are as a
person, and what you are proud of, including your values. One
such non-negotiable for me was to attempt to have meals at the
table as a family. This does not happen every night since we
have activities, or work during supper time, but we strive to do
that as much as possible. Other non negotiables may include:

- Never talk bad about my partner to others, and vice versa.
- Any purchase over $500, we will consult each other...
- Will not get between him and his parents during difficult conversations...

My Bold & Brave Diary...

What are your non-negotiables? If you are having a tough time coming up with some, think of your values that you listed in Chapter 1. Line up your non-negotiables with your values. Do they line up? What might these say about you? What is really important to you in your home?

_____

_____

_____

_____

_____

Once Ross and his wife completed this, they spoke about their lists, and compared notes. They learned new things about each other and realized that their lack of communication was hindering their relationship in more ways than one. They didn't understand each other's values and desires for their little family. In the end, they decided to try to stay together... an ending that no amount of money could ever buy!

Key takeaways:

1. Start the money conversation by taking a free online money course, if money is not a comfortable topic for discussions.
2. Financial problems are a symptom of something bigger.
3. Use the 80/20 rule to get adjusted to an equitable way to handle money.
4. Put your relationship, the third entity, ahead of yourself and your partner. Make the relationship the most valuable part of your life's wealth.
5. Money is the symptom of something else going on in the relationship.

CHAPTER SIX

S-E-X

*"Balls are weak and sensitive. If you really wanna get tough,
grow a vagina. Those things really take a pounding!"*
—BETTY WHITE—

What does sex mean to you? Is it important in your relationship? How often are you intimate with your partner? Do you like to call it making love? Or perhaps doing it, fornicating, fooling around, screwing, or copulating? Are you frigid, or do we have a dusty cobweb situation, covering your begonia (code for vagina)? (cue crickets chirping.)

Don't worry, we'll figure this out together...keep reading.

This question comes up repeatedly from couples I work with: "How many times a week should we be having sex?" And while I may be the expert on relationships, I am not an expert on your libidos! But you are. So, if you ever find yourself in front of a therapist who tells you, "Thou shalt have sex with thy wife or husband every day at 2:00 pm" as mentioned in the Kamasutra Chapter 6:9; (just kidding, that would be too perfect), please run!

No one knows how often you and your mate should do the deed. You both have to decide this for yourselves. More sex isn't always the answer. Sometimes, sex once a month can be enough because it's that good! However, the frequency of being intimate isn't the problem, it's a symptom. It could be a symptom of something much larger. There is no prescription for sex or the amount of sex that will fix the intimacy issues in a relationship. Usually, if there is a problem in the bedroom, there is a problem within the relationship.

Many believe that sex is the way we show love to one another; therefore, if there's no sex, then there's no relationship. And that would be...WRONG. You can still have a relationship that's fulfilling and emotionally connected without actual sexual intercourse. But sex sure helps to keep it close and interesting. We can show love to one another in many ways. Gifts, kindness, words of adoration, etc., are all ways of showing love to your partner. But, you can also use those things out of spite and anger; for example, providing a sarcastic gift may evoke strong emotions. We're abundantly aware that sex can be dirty, perverse, exploitative, illegal, repulsive, and used as a "weapon." In other words, it can be used to manipulate and hurt others. Sex can be used for power. Sex can be perverted and twisted. Sex can be bought and sold.

Sex is complicated.

Do you know anyone who withholds sex from their partner? Perhaps won't get down and dirty unless the dishwasher is clean and unloaded? Unfortunately, I hear this a lot as well. I have met more women than men who believe that this is acceptable in their relationship; that it's ok for their partner to *earn* sex by doing what the woman wants. "You don't do anything around here. I pick up after you, clean the house, and cook. And what do I get? I'm not about to give you sex until you start giving *me* something." Maybe you've heard this statement before, or you're realizing that you say this yourself. It's similar to saying, "I'm not inviting you to my birthday party because you didn't give me your lunch money at recess." Am I getting across to you? This is not a game between the two of you, and sex is not made for women to give to men if they earn it. Sex is so much better than that. But if you are using it like ammo, you have a bit of work to do. Read on...

Sex can be a form of intimacy; but it's not the only way to create intimacy. Sex is often thought of as a necessary part of a loving relationship. But there are many relationships that thrive, and are full of love and intimacy, but contain no sex at all. Wait, what? Intimacy without sex? I thought intimacy *was* sex, right? WRONG again.

Intimacy can be described as a close emotional bond between two loving partners. Intimacy can exist by just staring into each other's eyes with love and adoration. Is this something you're able to do? Most couples find this much more difficult than hopping in the sac for a quickie!

So why is sex such a hot topic? How did it come to be such a central part of a relationship?

Back in the "olden days," sex was focused on procreation, not recreation so much. Mind you, if you go to Pompeii, Italy, you will see evidence of recreational sex all over the village that dates back to 80 AD, when Mount Vesuvius erupted and covered the brothel laden town with molten lava and ash. Once it was uncovered, many years later, brothels with carvings of penises were all over the stone town. Stone beds (ouch) and graffiti of the sexual organs were prominent. If you were born in Pompeii, you may have been a part of an era that used sex for both procreation and recreation. If you were born into an Irish Catholic family, there may have been many babies, large families, and no birth control. One's upbringing can impact their view on sex, including the purpose of it. Sex for the sole reason of enjoyment has a history of being seen as sinful in many religions. For example, sex before marriage was a no-no, and if you decided to "do it," you would burn in hell for the rest of your existence, according to some religions. It might not be worth eternity for a few minutes of pleasure (or seconds, for others). Sex for pleasure, unfortunately, continues to be seen as sinful in some countries. In countries such as Ethiopia, there are many tribal groups that perform female genital mutilation (fgm). This would cancel out any ability for a woman to enjoy sex. Often, this practice is done without sanitary conditions and without anaesthesia. Unfortunately, this continues to be a common practice in many countries, and the practice of female genital mutilation continues to exist in far too many places. This disturbing practice resets us quickly, and can ground us in realizing that we have choices around intimacy and sex in North America.

So, what were you taught as a child? Did you grow up in a place that pushed procreation, recreation or both?

My Bold & Brave Diary...

How have your views on sex evolved within your own lifetime? What was taught to you at a young age? What were your experiences with sex? Take a few moments to jot down some answers to these questions:

_____

_____

_____

_____

_____

_____

_____

_____

_____

_____

_____

_____

_____

_____

_____

_____

_____

THE STORY OF DENVER AND TINA

Once upon a time, there was a man and a woman who were young and madly in love. It was like a fairytale love story. They had a fulfilled life ahead of them and couldn't wait to start their journey. Not long after meeting one another, they enjoyed the most beautiful wedding. It was the wedding Tina had imagined since she was a little girl. Denver went along with it. He didn't care what colours she chose, or where they would be married. He just wanted to spend the rest of his life with her.

The wedding came with a massive price tag though, and so did their new mortgage. They had to have the three bedroom home, with granite countertops, and the double oven. It was a beautiful home, but came at a cost. The first five years of marriage was harder than they'd anticipated. Tina thought it would be a good idea to go on a holiday, to bring back the romance and rekindle why they'd gotten married in the first place. So they had a wonderful European vacation, full of excursions, and virtually no stress. They made love every chance they had, and the connection was exactly what Tina had hoped for. As a result, they had a little bundle of joy that surprised them nine months later! A bundle for which they hadn't planned. But, they were excited and hopeful that this would be a new chapter for them, one that would help their marriage, or so they thought.

Their bundle of joy kept them busy for many years. There were diapers, sleepless nights, and debt up to their eyeballs. To their surprise, a second bundle arrived soon after. Now, they had a family of 5: husband, wife, two children, and their debt. Tina and Denver had recognized the trouble with their connection many years prior, but thought vacations and babies would aid in feeling closer to each other. Sound familiar?

Denver and Tina came to see me to receive help with their relationship of twelve years. They were considering having a third child and Tina was worried about bringing a new baby into a dynamic that was already chaotic.

So what brings you in today?

I'm really worried about not being able to manage my life if we have another baby! Denver is always working, I work part time, and our kids have so many activities that I'm a virtual taxi service. We're hardly managing now, let alone taking care of a third! Every morning I'm late getting to work, and I'm exhausted before the end of the day. The kids need so much of my attention, and so does Denver. I'm just not sure how to continue this way.

Wow Tina, this sounds like a lot for you to manage. How does it feel right now, saying all of this in front of Denver?

Like he's going to be mad at me and will keep me up late, she said gingerly.

Ok. Denver, how did it feel to hear this from Tina?

I don't understand her! She has such a great life. We have lots of nice things, she's satisfied daily, and she has all this time off. I'm so confused by her. She cries a lot, and I try to make her feel better but it doesn't really help because she just starts crying again when we are done!

When you are done, what exactly? I asked.

When we're done having sex at night.

Oh, ok, so what I'm hearing is that you have sex to feel better? Is that right, Denver?

Well yeah, of course. I don't get it. Every night we have sex but it isn't making anything better.

At this point, I didn't get it either. Was I hearing them correctly? They have sex *every* night? *Oy vey!* That can be physically demanding, particularly for a couple with young and active children (not to mention the potential of irritating the "begonia"!).

Sorry, Denver, did you say you have sex every night?

Well, yes! That's what my parents did, and we do too.

I was biting my lip because my mouth would have fallen open in shock; something therapists should try to avoid!

I see. Tina, what about you? How do you feel about sex?

Well, I like it; but not twice a day.

Twice a day? (Still biting my lip.)

Yeah, this is one of our problems. Denver expects it when we wake up and before we fall asleep. I just don't have the energy! It's become a chore!

Working with Denver and Tina was eye-opening for me. As a therapist, we do not give advice, or try to change our clients' minds. Rather, we encourage our clients to explore their emotions, which provides a doorway to change. Were they having sex twice a day for emotional connection? For intimacy? What was sex being used for?

Through more discussion and sharing, it was discovered that Denver had low self esteem. He had figured out a way to fill the void of connection along with his low self worth, by using sex. The void would go away temporarily, but a few hours later, he would need to fulfill it again (and fill it again he did!). This void can truly only be filled by an emotional connection. But for Denver to have an emotional connection, he would have to learn how to be vulnerable. And to be vulnerable, he would need enough confidence in himself to do so. I was curious about the quality of connection Denver may have felt, which was short lived.

Fast forward twenty years and Tina and Denver found themselves with two older children, and a child who had never grown up named Debt. They never ended up having a third child. At this point, twice a day sex was not happening anymore! As a matter of fact, it wasn't happening at all. Denver was still suffering from low self esteem and low self worth. To top it all off, Denver had taken up online gambling. Since sex was finito, he found another way to help him fill his void; and in doing so, was filled with debt instead of emotional connection.

They were both working forty hours + per week, exhausted by the time they got home, then had to do their household chores, make dinner, clean up, and take care of Denver's ageing mother. They were on a hamster wheel and couldn't get caught up. If they took a day or two off work to catch up on sleep, then the bills wouldn't get paid, they would be behind on them, and behind on their chores/laundry/care for mom, then the anxiety would kick in, which would make them more exhausted... Sound familiar?

Tina was lonely in the relationship and was resentful towards Denver and life in general. She had spent twenty years raising their two children, working a job she couldn't stand, and now was caring for her mother in law, who she really couldn't stand to be around. Tina had lost herself and was totally stuck. She gave herself to her family like many women do, and did not pay any attention to herself. She put herself last, instead of meeting her own needs. There was never enough time to do much for herself. The hamster wheel didn't allow for it. She could never catch a break! Again, does this sound familiar?

All of a sudden, they were 45 years old, with a few more rolls and a few more wrinkles. Sleep apnea kept Denver in the spare room while Tina slept alone in their bedroom. Most nights were sleepless, worrying about money, losing their house, being fat, and drinking too much. Conflict arose from the stresses in their lives, including the bills and parenting teenagers. Tina and Denver both felt alone, overwhelmed, and hopeless. They had gone through the last fifteen years in a total blur. They lost themselves and their own identities amid the busyness of their lives, and the financial commitment to their creditors. They lost what they thought they had built together. Both felt unfulfilled. As a result, there was an emptiness that pervaded their every day. An emptiness that couldn't be filled... until *one* of them tasted something that felt like fulfillment...

Tina worked at an accounting office which was equivalently as exciting as watching paint dry. She had a disagreement with the photocopier, in which she won. So, a phone call to the repair man was made due to the damage. Not long after the phone call, loving eyes gazed upon her like she had never felt before. Stan the Man, a handsome photocopy repair guy, would frequent Tina's office. She quickly noticed his smile and Tina would jam the copier on purpose, hoping Stan would come by to repair it. She felt a flutter in her chest, and a warmth within her loins, when she witnessed his muscular arms lift the xerox ink cartridges with such grace. She hadn't felt that flutter in a long time. Her husband hadn't been paying much attention to her lately, but Stan the Man sure had. He wore tight blue industrial type polyester pants that held his buns ever so tightly. She was hoping he needed to access the bottom drawer, to unjam the 8 1/2 inches x 11 inches she had rammed in there earlier in the day. Tina's body was becoming hot and ripe. She was nervous to go over to him, but she couldn't resist. Tina inched behind Stan and grabbed...

Ok, enough of that. Let's get back on track, shall we? Though a little burlesque, the scenario above provides a snapshot of a moment when the emptiness Tina had felt in her relationship was exacerbated due to an unforgettable distraction and a need to fill an emotional void. There were moments that sucked her in (*that's what she said...*) like the plague. The rest is history.

That was the first day of Tina's affair, and a story that so many others share in their 40s and 50s, who are seeking fulfillment. Regrettably, that fulfillment is often an illusion, is short lived and full of regret. This is one example of how easy it is to go astray in an unfulfilled relationship. This is one example of the current epidemic of affairs amongst women in their 40s. (Not to say that it's any different amongst men.) The void, as mentioned in chapter one, can be extremely debilitating. A lack of fulfillment and connection can drive one's behaviour to lengths that would surprise the faintest of hearts. fulfillment through emotional connection is powerful. A lack of that fulfillment can be even more powerful. This is one of the reasons why infidelity is on the rise in our society. We live in a society in which many people feel unfulfilled. And while the symptoms include one's job, partner, physique, time, etc., they are all just masking the reality that an emotional void is present.

Infidelity can come in many forms. From having a mistress or mister on the side, to a spending account, lying and cheating can erode a relationship faster than toxic waste in a garden. I want you to ask yourself though, what happened before the infidelity? Whether it happened to you or your partner, there is always a reason for every behaviour. Whether a toddler has a tantrum for a toy or a man takes home a woman from a bar, there is a purpose behind the behaviour. Perhaps you are having an affair and are questioning if you should leave your partner for your new squeeze? I have heard many times that affairs often happen with someone who's totally "not my type;" that the philandering partner isn't necessarily attracted to the person with whom they're having the affair, but that something just came over them that can't quite be explained. Perhaps an adrenaline rush? But I have generally suspected over the years in this profession that the reason is due to loneliness and a void within. The void is nearly always created by the lack of an emotional connection with one's partner.

Often, the emotional connection is missing due to unresolved trauma, past relationships, lack of self love, and/or a lack of self awareness. So, if you map that backwards, you will see that doing the work of understanding yourself, your flaws and all, excavating past traumas and past relationships, then working with your partner to improve the emotional connection, will create a stable and secure loving emotional connection that will be bulletproof and affair-proof. This work will most often foster an unbreakable form of intimacy which will strengthen your emotional connection and your bond together.

THE BOTTOM LINE UNFILTERED

A lack of emotional connection is a significant reason many people seek fulfillment elsewhere. When individuals feel disconnected or unvalued in their relationships, they often turn to external sources to fill the void. This can manifest in various ways, such as affairs, substance abuse, excessive shopping, gambling, or seeking validation through casual encounters. These actions are attempts to fill a deep-seated emotional gap, but they often provide only temporary relief. The thrill or distraction they offer is short-lived because the activity filling the void lacks true meaning and depth. Our spirits crave genuine, meaningful connection and fulfillment, which these superficial pursuits cannot provide.

Reciprocal love plays a crucial role in this context. When love is given and returned, it creates a powerful emotional bond that fulfills our innate need for connection and belonging. This mutual exchange of love generates a sense of security and value, filling the emotional void in a way that fleeting pleasures cannot. When a partner reciprocates love, it reinforces our sense of self-worth and nurtures our emotional well-being. Unlike temporary fixes, the fulfilment derived from reciprocal love is deeply rooted and long-lasting. It satisfies our need for intimacy and connection, grounding us in a meaningful relationship that fosters growth, support, and shared joy.

In contrast, when love is not reciprocated, or when there is a lack of emotional connection, individuals may feel isolated and unappreciated. This emotional emptiness drives the search for fulfilment through unmeaningful means. However, these substitutes cannot match the quality of fulfilment that comes from a loving, reciprocal relationship. Our spirits are not designed to be satisfied by empty, momentary distractions. True fulfilment arises from meaningful forces—like the mutual exchange of love with a partner—that resonate with our deepest emotional needs. Thus, the enduring fulfilment found in reciprocal love far surpasses any temporary fix, providing a solid foundation for emotional health and happiness.

Key takeaways:

1. Sex can have multiple meanings.
2. When there is a lack of emotional connection, many will seek fulfilment elsewhere.
3. Reciprocal love will create a deep loving emotional connection.

CHAPTER 7

Fear & Compassion

*"Scars remind us of where we've been. They
don't have to dictate where we're going."*

—DAVID ROSSI OF CRIMINAL MINDS—

Now that you've learned *how* you got here, and have learned
new strategies to create the relationship you've always wanted,
it's time to apply these skills to your current relationship. But
first, let's talk about your mattress! How is it treating you? It
is a fancy pillow top? A twenty year-old foam piece of crap
with coils sticking into parts you didn't know you had? Or
perhaps you have the Craftmatic Adjustable Bed, the same
one that was advertised during *The Price Is Right*, throughout
your childhood. Either way, think about how it would feel
to change your mattress. Just imagine: You buy the perfect
mattress you've always dreamed of, only to find out, the new
mattress is like a lunchbag let down. There is no groove for
your bum, no spot for Spike the dog to sleep in, and definitely
no familiar creaky sound when you shift slightly to the left.
This sounds scary! Have you ever noticed how many mattress
stores there are? Tons!! How many times do people need to
buy a mattress? How do these stores stay in business? Well, I
guess people must be replacing their mattresses much more
than I thought. But I, for one, feel scared to buy a new one,
even though I've dreamt of that Craftmatic Adjustable Bed
since Bob Barker said "Help control the pet population folks!"

Now I want you to imagine that a mattress represents your relationship with your partner. Does staying in the same place in your relationship feel like the lumpy piece of foam on your bed, after twenty years of sleeping in the same spot? No movement, no change, just comfortably uncomfortable on the old mattress. It's scary to go to Costco to buy a new bed, isn't it? You risk having to face sleepless nights, tossing and turning, and trying to work on creating a new impression in the mattress. The unknown is often feared and can keep you stuck. But what often precipitates a significant change is a metal spring, jamming in your back, which in turn creates movement to a new mattress. Imagine each spring represents different relationship injuries or difficult situations you've encountered over the course of your courtship. One spring is the heart attack you had when your cousin's Buffalo Wings were far from mild, the other spring represents the time you got fired for jamming the photocopier with Stan the Man.

The same principle applies in relationships: only when the comfortable becomes very uncomfortable will a couple seek change. Just like improving your sleep, self improvements require work, dedication, attention and perhaps most importantly, awareness. Though the process isn't always enjoyable, not doing it will hurt much more. Evolving as a couple may move you into foreign territory that includes learning unknown things about yourself, your partner and your relationship.

I will never forget when I was twenty something, my mom told me that she and my father had switched sides of the bed. My mom, the daredevil, said she was tired of sleeping on the same side of the bed, for thirty years, and wanted to try out "the other side" for herself. This very daring move in their long standing and loving marriage may sound like a miniscule decision to you, but it can also be seen as a step towards change in their marriage. The mattress, and switching sides, are metaphors for moving forward and changing the way the marriage has always been. This may sound easy, but if it was, we wouldn't have such a high divorce rate on our hands. Take a moment and consider how you might implement a new change or a new strategy that you have learned in this book. Often, we fail to realize how much we may impact what's happening in our relationship. Yes, it's much easier to blame someone else than to look within ourselves as a contributor to the problem. But no one said it would be easy. It's far easier to stay where we are, so we can avoid the uncomfortable feelings that can come with self reflection and improving our relationships. Plus, the unknown of how it will play out, can keep us frozen with fear.

Fear can be a relentless force, keeping us stuck and stifling the warrior within. It shows up repeatedly, immobilizing us and feeding a timid ego that resists acknowledging its shortcomings. But this resistance makes sense—facing our fears requires vulnerability, trust, and a willingness to confront what's often hidden. Fear is a signal, a sign that there is something within us that needs work. It can be a gateway to growth if we learn to see it as an opportunity rather than a barrier. When we face our fears head-on, we enter a state of perpetual awareness and self-expansion.

Identifying fear can be challenging, especially when it hides behind other emotions. For instance, in a difficult relationship where communication feels impossible, you might feel apprehensive, worried, or overwhelmed about bringing up your concerns. To uncover the fear beneath these feelings, ask yourself, "What might this say about me?" This question often reveals a deeper fear, like the fear of rejection or not being good enough. Such fears can trap us in a cycle of avoidance, leading to a lack of communication and deeper disconnection.

However, compassion can be the antidote. As the gateway to love, compassion involves a desire to help someone heal, including yourself. It fosters a positive energy flow that promotes movement and change. When we approach fear with compassion, we allow ourselves the grace to confront our vulnerabilities and the courage to grow. Recognizing fear and facing it with compassion can break the cycle, opening us up to more honest communication and deeper connections. In this process, we transform fear from an obstacle into a path toward personal growth and a more fulfilling relationship.

My Bold & Brave Diary...

Let's examine your fear. How does it show up? How does it keep you stuck in the same pattern that erodes your relationship? I wonder how it feels to even think about uncovering what isn't known to you, and to do the work required. Does that create waves in your stomach? Does your heart rate increase?

_____

_____

_____

_____

_____

_____

_____

_____

_____

_____

_____

_____

_____

_____

_____

My fear is an ugly, bright orange prickly blob that sneaks in like a bad smell that takes over my entire environment. This blob leads me to spiral out of control, which only stops once I have talked myself off the ledge. But this part is tough; my fears are real and have weighed me down in more ways than one. As well, they have affected my life and have stopped me from doing things I otherwise would have done. The unknown is scary and the daunting task of facing it can lead people to stay in the stuck spots. If you start the process of uncovering the unknown, it means that you may become accountable to what lurks there. You'll have to face the demon once it's revealed. Are you ready for that?

These are the moments when many clients cancel their appointments. In therapy, by the 4th or 5th session, clients have generally entered the unknown territory, which permeates the room. This is a pivotal moment when one decides if they will dive deeply into the work they have to do or lie down in the mattress indent, and try to ignore the coils sticking into their back. This is where the work would generally start, and the challenge of facing aspects of themselves and their relationships can scare them off. Facing the unknown provokes fear, and fear is a beast to many.

One of my fears includes the fear of criticism, which can show up daily. When I was in my thirties, I remember when a colleague found out I played the piano. He needed a keyboardist for some gigs, to which I adamantly said, "No way," when he asked me to sub in. He was relentless though, and somehow convinced me to go to a practice. I remember how much I loved it, and was hooked. But I was petrified before I eventually did it, and tried to get out of it. Being in a band was on my bucket list, and this was an opportunity to fulfil that desire, but it was just too scary. In spite of having an honours degree in music, when he asked me to play three chords in a I-IV-V-I progression (easiest progression there is), it scared the crap out of me. This made no sense. But oftentimes nothing makes sense when it comes to fear. In other words, you're playing irrational. I felt the fear in my stomach and chest, and the fear of criticism and fear of not being good enough. It was all valid enough for me to want to stay away from my dream. Can you relate?

If fear is one of the reasons why people shy away from taking risks outside of their comfort zones like joining a band or taking the initiative to improve their relationships, perhaps this is why we have a culture in North America in which some people fall into patterns of negativity, complaining, and stagnation. To put it bluntly, instead of leaning into the fear, we become the fear, and fear can be nasty. Not facing the fear, complaining, lashing outwards, lashing inwards, finding distractions: they're all coping mechanisms. And they all keep us from achieving our full potential.

Often, people feel trapped by fear and overwhelmed by life's challenges. This often leads to a belief that they are victims of circumstances beyond their control. They may struggle to see potential pathways for change or feel overwhelmed by the prospect of taking action. Others might find a sense of validation or camaraderie in commiserating with others who share their misery. Self-loathing and embracing victimhood can easily become a habit at this point, which can reinforce a cycle of complaining, without resolution; also known as *misery loves company*. I'm sure you can remember a recent time when someone wouldn't stop complaining... "Blah bla Blah bla blah..." It's like watching paint dry, on your own, in a dark room, on your birthday. The entire world is waiting for you to come celebrate, but you're stuck listening to a broken record of complaints! As a therapist, I often listen to complaints. I get paid well to reframe some of these complaints, and to bring out the *why* behind the complaints. Interestingly, studies show that if you allow someone to go on complaining, without stopping or interrupting them, the average time for which they will complain will be three minutes. Try it! Ask someone to let out all their complaints without fueling their fire. Bring a stopwatch.

Lashing inward is what children tend to do, to cope with difficult situations when it comes to their parents. Children see themselves as flawed, rather than becoming aware of their parents' shortcomings. This behaviour and these beliefs stay with them into their adulthood, and often, the only way to undo these beliefs is through therapy, understanding and healing. For some, the protection they create, like a hard shell, works for them in the sense that they don't have to feel the pain and agony they've accumulated. Whatever coping mechanism is chosen, (drugs, alcohol, sex, exercise, food, cigarettes, work, sleep; to name a few...) provides the temporary illusion of escaping from the physical and mental anguish. However, it often comes back stronger after each bender. As well, not working through the anguish means they miss out on the beautiful emotional connection with others—and with themselves. If these coping strategies don't take away the anguish, then the body can go to the next level of avoiding the anguish, which is called *dissociation*, and can be described as the body separating itself from the mind. It's a protective strategy of the mind designed to keep someone from experiencing psychological and physical distress. We all dissociate somehow. Think about moments when you are "spaced out" or are "in your own world." It's almost like a break from consciousness. In fact, it truly is! Dissociation is a natural way for the body and mind to protect itself when it's in danger. However, when triggered after all the danger is gone, the body can still dissociate since the trauma can be stuck in the mind. It isn't until we treat the underlying trauma, that dissociative symptoms decrease. So as I said earlier, we have to know what's *behind* the fear, and not just address the fear itself.

My Bold & Brave Diary...

Are you able to identify your fears? Remember, start with how you feel, then what might that say about you?

_____

_____

_____

_____

How do those fears keep you stuck or try to control you?

_____

_____

_____

_____

What are your fears when you imagine yourself talking to your partner about your feelings, and the truths you feel? What might happen?

_____

_____

_____

_____

_____

What could you be giving up if you address those
feelings and the fears that accompany them?

_____

_____

_____

_____

What could you risk by not addressing your fears
and feelings?

_____

_____

_____

_____

At this point, you may be thinking, *Jennifer, you don't know
me! I have so many meaningful relationships!* If that is you,
congratulations! You are a part of the minority of people who
get to experience true emotional experiences. But if this is you
and you completed the My Bold & Brave Diary with some
"a-ha" moments, then you may need to dig a little deeper in this
area to see how connected you truly are in your relationships.
Remember, I am cheering you on to get there! And if you aren't
quite there, then remember: It will all make sense as to why
you aren't totally emotionally connected yet. After all, this is
your journey at *your* pace.

The ability to bond with another or show empathy and warmth is very difficult as an adult if you were yelled at and hit for making noise as a child. If your mother didn't notice you or wasn't available enough when you were a child, you will work hard to get noticed. Many of these children who become adults are known as the perfectionists of the world and are often stricken with anxiety. They see a world full of people who appear to have themselves' together and see themselves as not good enough or never good enough. The truth is, the person you saw in the line up today getting a double double at Timmy's, who looks like her s**t doesn't stink... Well, let me tell ya...light a match! It's often easier to fight the inside voice about ourselves than to listen to it, and work with it. Our inner parts (also known as *Ego States*) will never be enough until we learn that our internal working model of ourselves is jaded. The inaccuracies of our beliefs need to be revealed, understood, grieved, then healed. The symptoms of not feeling good enough will continue to show up day after day until the cause is exposed. Only then may we create a new internal working model, which can be a struggle in itself—but is well worth the while.

THE STORY OF CHIP AND SHELLEY

One such client I worked with grew up in a difficult home, full of avoidance, mistrust, and a survival of the fittest mentality. She remembers having money stolen from her piggy bank by her mother, who would drink herself silly, and who wouldn't notice when Shelley left the house for days at a time. They were in a small rural town in the prairies of Canada, where "Children were supposed to be seen and not heard." One session sticks out in my mind, in which I recall Shelley telling me a story that still makes me shudder at the thought of what she endured as a young child. Shelley was in a relationship with Chip, who was a police officer, and who had a habit of yelling when he was angry. He was also in attendance.

Chip, tell me what happens for you when you feel the anger you've described.

Well, I feel mad.

Yes, go on...

(It's easier to be angry than to show hurt and fear. Often men have three emotions with which they identify: mad, glad, sad. But there is so much more in there!)

Yeah, mad and angry. I'm pissed off when Shelley mentions how the bills have piled up. I don't want to talk about it.

Why not?

Because! Who wants to talk about money unless they have it!?

Ok, I hear you...it has a negative feeling attached to it?

Yes, my last girlfriend expected me to pay for everything, and I went totally broke because of her.

So, you have some bad memories of how you spent your money while dating your ex girlfriend. Is that right?

Well, yeah, I guess so. I felt like I didn't have a choice with her. So I promised myself after that, that I would never let another woman into my finances. No matter what.

Ok, makes sense. You were really hurt and taken advantage of. So, you figured out a way to protect yourself for the future.

Yes.

Ok, thank you. Shelley, what comes up for you when you hear Chip say he doesn't want to open up about finances with you?

I feel like I'm not worth it. Like he has made up his mind.

Ok, what feeling is attached to that?

I feel alone, confused, and sad...really sad... This isn't going to work if we can't work together on our future goals, which have to include finances.

So, you are sad, feeling alone, and like you don't matter enough for Chip to open up about finances. Is that right?

Yes, and no. I feel like he doesn't think I am worth the time and effort it would take for him to get over his last relationship, and move on. If he did, finances wouldn't be such an issue anymore.

Ok. Thank you Shelley. Chip, how are you doing? Does that bring up anything for you?

Sure does. I don't want her feeling like she's not important enough. I love her, and want to be with her. But when I think about the finances and talking about it, yuck. I feel gross inside, and I want to be left alone.

Chip, this makes sense! You are programmed to protect yourself after being hurt! Running away and being left alone would protect you and your finances. But it would also keep you from having the loving, secure relationship you said you want with Shelley. What is stopping you from staying and talking about it?

Well, I am worried, like I said earlier.

Behind that worry, could there be anything else there? I'm curious, is there some fear there?

Hmm, fear of what?

I'm not sure, but I'm wondering if there is some fear of being hurt again. What do you think?

Yeah, I could see that. That would really suck. I was pretty hurt in the past.

Yes, can you turn to Shelley and tell her that?

And so, Chip shared how scared he was that he would endure more hurt. He wasn't fearful of Shelley per se, but of what could happen if he shared his finances again.

Then, it was time to deepen the emotion with Shelley.

Shelley, tell me what comes up for you when you hear Chip share his feelings about his fear?

I feel bad for him...and sad. What a bitch she was. I would never do that to him. I too know what it feels like to be betrayed by someone you love. My mother did that to me.

Tell me...

She made some horrible decisions. She would steal from me and my siblings so she could buy her next bottle. She would go on benders for days. I would answer the phone when the school would call in the morning, and justify my absence, pretending I was her, and then would go on my bike around the neighbourhood with a friend down the street. We both had parents who were addicts. Her mom was a sex worker too. She had a double whammy.

Oh Shelley, you must have seen many things a child should never see. I am so sorry.

I did. I will never forget when my mom was so pissed off at my dad, who had already been dead for at least a year, when she found out he cashed in his life insurance and spent the money at the casino; losing it all. I remember hearing her yelling at no one, slurring her words and calling him every name in the book while frantically searching the old bureau in the main room. I was watching from the closet, where I was hiding because I was supposed to be in school. Then, I saw her with an envelope that had a bunch of baggies in it. All I remember is her saying, "Now what are you going to do? Smoke more drugs? Huh?" Then she said, "Goodbye deadbeat!" That's when I heard her flush the toilet.

My sister told me years later that my dad was cremated and his remains were in a yellow manila envelope in small bags—five of them, one for each child. It was his birthday and she had arranged

for his ashes to be sprinkled in the fields where he grew up. It was
at that moment I realized what my mother had done.

Shelley grew up to be a well loved teacher, who was instrumental in helping countless children in the depths of poverty just like she had been. She found purpose through her pain, which helped her heal from the horrible memories and moments that she shouldn't have had as a child. Shelley was neglected as a child, and was fearful of having money hidden from her in her current relationship, and any secrets relating to finances. Not only did her mother steal from her, and flush her father's ashes down the toilet in a fit of drunken rage, but her dad was a compulsive gambler who put the family at risk many times. Shelley had a *disorganized attachment style*, and was able to heal from the many injuries of her past. Shelley and Chip ended up taking a finance course together to start the dialogue. This client was a very memorable one for me; she was the epitome of resilience and strength. I felt privileged to be a part of her journey of healing and personal growth.

THE BOTTOM LINE UNFILTERED

If fear can keep us so stuck, then we need to dig deep to figure out the *why* within ourselves. Just as Chip and Shelley discovered their own internal fears that may have been impacted by neglect from their caregivers or a misguided partner, you too must learn where your fear stems from. Your past will inform your future, and can help you get unstuck so you can move past the fear.

But in doing that, have compassion for yourself and for the work you're embarking upon. You are strong, and deserve to sleep on a comfortable mattress. Recognize that you too deserve compassion and grace, just as you might give to a friend that you are caring for in the same situation. As we practise self compassion, the process of facing our fears can become a little more manageable. Practising self compassion can help us move forward without any lingering guilt or other unhelpful feelings. Look at how courageous and strong you are. There is only one way now, which is forward. With self-compassion, you will be free from self loathing and will be empowered to achieve the badass relationship you have worked so hard to have!

Key takeaways:

1. Fear can keep us stuck.
2. To understand how to get unstuck, we must acknowledge the fear within us and heal from it.

CHAPTER 8

The Ten Relationship Commandments

By this point in your reading, you've gained a multitude of tools, suggestions, examples, and exercises from which to learn and apply, if you choose. Perhaps you didn't like any of the suggestions in the book. Fine; no problem. Thanks for your $20. My last words to you are: "Your way is still not working, so find a new one..." On the flip side, maybe you loved my book. Still, thanks for the $20 and the 5 star review (hint, hint). So, my sincere last few words for the readers who didn't care for this book are: Remember as you move forward with your new tools that it doesn't have to be all or nothing, black or white. The grey area is a perfect place to be. Change doesn't happen overnight, and it certainly didn't take one night to get you to this present moment. It's a process, which you need to trust. Yes, the overused metaphor is correct: trust the process (insert eye roll). Continue forward and stop creating from a retrospective viewpoint. Although the past informs your future, it doesn't have to mirror it. It can merely be a reflection of where you came from and how far you've come!

For the readers who loved this book, read on! (And please remember to look for my next book called, *What Your Therapist Can't Say...PARENTS' EDITION.*) I am sure you've also come to some interesting conclusions about yourself and what you've noticed as you've looked in the mirror and evaluated yourself.

More on that in the next and final chapter. But for now, let's have a look at how and why some of the tips may be helpful with the help of Roy and Tasha...

THE STORY OF ROY AND TASHA

So tell me a little bit about what brought you in today?

Well, I am tired of Roy's attitude and just don't know how much longer I can take it! He drives me crazy with his big ass ego, flaunting it all over his socials. So irritating and cringy!

Ok Tasha, are you able to tell me how that feels for you, right here, right now?

Yeah, like a piece of s**Bt, he comments on other women's posts, or stares at other women's tits when we're out together. It's so rude.

I can see that is very upsetting for you. Are you able to tell me how you feel though? Bring it back to you, and how it lands for you.

Ok, well, I am embarrassed. As if I can't control my boyfriend.

Um, can you explain?

Well, my last boyfriend would worship the ground I walked on. He would do whatever I asked him to do. I liked that. It felt good.

Ok, why did it feel good for you?

Well, he was right there when I needed him but I could also tell him to go away when I was sick of him.

Hmm, ok. Thank you for sharing that. I wonder if-

Roy interjected- *For sh*t sake Tasha, how could you bring him up. You're such a bitch.*

I interrupted him, *Roy, I hear you, but can we slow down for a moment? Tasha, can we stay with the moment and just pause for a second as well? Can we all take a deep breath and try to reset together?*

Sigh- Ok, I'll try.. But I am tired of his LDS... Tasha rolled her eyes while she said this.

WTF Tasha, What are you talking about?? Roy said.

Oh Roy, you know what I mean...you have Little Dick Syndrome. You try to make up for your little dick with your really big mouth and attitude.

At this point, Roy got up and said some choice words to Tasha, looked at me and said he was done with her.

Tasha ran after him, and I have not heard from either of them since...

A part of my job is to de-escalate any escalation in the room. Generally, this goes really well. This was a first for me, and I had to do some self reflection on both my practice, and my own ego. *How did this happen? I failed this couple.* After a good night's sleep, I realised that I gave my best and that the couple may not have been ready for couples work. Either way, I also realised how valuable rules could have been had this couple followed even a few of them. For example, no name calling. It's hurtful and doesn't get anyone anywhere. We've all done it, at one point in our life, and hopefully, have learned from that experience. Usually the name calling is coming from a place of hurt. Had Tasha said she was hurting, the session would have gone a totally different way. Instead, she responded in a protective mode and lashed outwards. Tasha could have also sought out some support with emotional regulation to help control her go-to emotional response of lashing outwards and hurting others.

Has your partner done anything similar to Roy and Tasha's behaviour towards each other? Have you? The My Bold & Brave Diary below may shed some light on some of your least proud moments in your relationship. Remember we are all human, and this is not for your suffering, but for your healing. It's designed to help you move forward and find some purpose out of the pain in these less than favourable moments.

My Bold & Brave Diary...

1. Write down all the things your partner has done to you that you just can't get past:

_____

_____

_____

_____

2. Now, write down anything that drives you crazy about your partner, that irks you:

_____

_____

_____

_____

3. Think about all of your own imperfections, that might drive them crazy (yes, you read that right; you are not perfect. Rather, perfectly imperfect...❤)

_____

_____

_____

_____

4. Now, burn this mofo (outside, in a safe place, with water nearby, no fire ban...etc...) or shred it! (not this book though, keep the book, maybe tear out this page...)

_____

_____

_____

_____

5. Reflect on what you would like to focus on now. Think about a few positives about your partner and yourself. What are you thankful for? How would your life change if you didn't have them tomorrow? Or you were not around tomorrow?

_____

_____

_____

_____

6. This is the reset for your future.

THE TEN COMMANDMENTS

Let's recap some of the top strategies I have seen work in relationships and the strategies I can't say in session but would love to offer to you! Check off the ones that you think would work for you. It's ok to disagree with this list, but commit to a few that may change the trajectory of your relationship path.

COMMANDMENT #1

- **Third entity:**

Think of your relationship as something that exists between the two of you. This is the third entity which should be protected, nurtured and loved, no matter what's happening (outside of abuse, of course). This is not easy, but necessary. You may need space to calm down at times, and will be a pro at this in other times. But keep this tenet in the forefront of your mind consistently, to guide you in being committed, even when it's hard.

COMMANDMENT #2

- **Be still together & find a community:**

Don't forget to enjoy the moments. As we chase tomorrow and plan for the future, stresses will always present themselves. Stop, plant your feet together, go for a walk, take pictures, or just be still. Lead with your heart, and the rest will follow.

Find a community of people who are living the life you want. Join a church, hobby group, coffee group, or simply reach out to someone you admire. We tend to gravitate to certain people in our lives. Have you ever heard that if you want to be a successful business owner, you should start hanging out with successful business owners? Well, this works really well for relationships, particularly if you search for people who already exhibit the traits that you aspire to embody, like positivity, love, and commitment.

COMMANDMENT #3

- **Take divorce off the table:**

STOP using it as a weapon! It is so unfair to throw this word around, especially during a conflict. In my profession, I see people who make decisions in the heat of the moment or the day after a trying argument. The impulsivity of breaking up with your partner in the moment is not helpful, and is a total hindrance to any positive movement in the relationship. Separation can't be taken lightly and should not be decided upon overnight because of a few instances. In other words, get rid of the "list" that you were keeping on your partner because it's only going to fuel your impulsivity and may foster reactiveness in your toughest moments. If separation or divorce is the next step, decide this after you have figured out your pattern as a couple. Do you remember chapter 4, where we learned about fighting the cycle that exists between you, instead of fighting each other? We all do this or have done it; it's often our go-to response when we are feeling alone, refused, or just plain annoyed. The cycle will follow you to your next relationship anyway, so you might as well get rid of it!

COMMANDMENT #4

- **Give your partner the benefit of the doubt & forgive them:**

I once worked with a couple where the husband couldn't trust his wife, despite her unwavering commitment to their family. No matter how much she gave, he always doubted her, believing others over her. Often, mental health struggles, personal insecurities, or life changes can block trust, and couples therapy alone may not be enough. Personal therapy may be needed to uncover underlying issues. In relationships, forgiveness plays a crucial role—it's not just about resolving conflict but also about giving someone the benefit of the doubt and truly letting go. Can you forgive and move forward without holding onto past grievances? True forgiveness means no longer using past mistakes as weapons, but instead choosing to rebuild trust and move ahead together.

COMMANDMENT #5

- **Standards (or boundaries) instead of barrier:**

One of the keys to a healthy relationship is to have the foundational attitude that you're partners and that you're on the same team. Being vulnerable is a wonderful way to collaborate, grow your relationship, and demonstrate a togetherness that's rooted in the spirit of partnership. We can't do a relationship alone. So ask yourself, "Are there unhealthy patterns of behaviour in our relationship?" Or are you just not showing grace for a few moments when your partner makes a mistake? Sometimes we must meet halfway to make it work. After all, we said "for richer or poorer, in sickness and in health," but we don't say, *unless it gets really hard, then I will bail on you.* That would definitely put an interesting spin on marriage ceremonies: *I love you with all my heart, unless you make me second-guess that love by being a total jerk. Oh, and if you do, I will make you pay with the silent treatment, but for richer or poorer, 'til death do us part, unless I first kill you in your sleep because I'm so angry at you and don't know how to talk to you, and I've lost all vulnerability because it got hard, I do.*

Is it going to be new boundaries together or is it going to be bye bye? Remember what boundaries are: they're not designed to control one another. Rather, they are designed to protect ourselves. When we use boundaries to keep others away, they are barriers. If used correctly, we protect ourselves and our emotional connection with others. Boundaries need to be created within all relationships. But in a marriage or a committed relationship, I'd like to think of them as standards that we hold near and dear. They don't necessarily have to be precisely in-line with one another's value systems, but they have to intersect them with love and respect.

COMMANDMENT #6

- **What is the intention?**

But you said you didn't want to go to the party.

Yes, but I didn't mean it that way, what I meant was that I didn't want to go out to party with

everyone...I don't mind going.

Well, you said you didn't want to go...

Above is a common argument of back and forth over what someone said. One partner is holding it against the other partner. Again, this is what children tend to do. Let's get to the intention behind the message. Perhaps the partner didn't get his words out right, or didn't get his point across the way he wanted to. Or perhaps the other partner only heard what they wanted to. Either way, ask what the intention is instead. This will get you clarity in the conversation, and will avoid a fight.

COMMANDMENT #7

- **ZERO worry/d*mn/f***s to Give**

A great strategy for lowering the amount of disturbances in your life and choosing your battles is to think about how many "worries" you have to give during the course of a day. You can even make a jar with the word "worries" (or any other word of your choice) on it, and put 10, 5, or any amount, in the jar. Every time you give away your energy or worry to an issue/problem, you have to give one up! Then, you only have 9 left. This strategy can put things into perspective and may encourage a more judicious perception on the size of the problem, at the moment.

COMMANDMENT #8

- **Humour & Sarcasm**

Can you laugh at yourself? I remember being so angry at my husband for not enjoying my cooking when we met. Now, I try not to cook too much since I know it's not one of my many talents! When I do, I stick to basic things and do my best not to burn it. I have come to terms with this; and over the last 20 years, I can finally laugh at myself when I have to throw out a whole meal.

Are you having fun together? Is life so serious you can't have a good laugh? Find ways to have fun together, and laugh. It is so good for the soul! Oh, and always laugh at your partner's jokes, no matter how stupid they are!! However, sarcasm is dangerous. Sarcasm is not humour; instead, it can often be a malicious way of getting your point across behind a "funny" comment. It's also known as "the protest of the weak." If you listen to sarcastic remarks from others, and take those comments at face value, believing them to be honest feelings, this statement will make sense to you! Have you ever heard, "oh, I'm just joking"? Oftentimes, people, especially children, will try to get their point across by using sarcastic "jokes." I call bulls**t. Say what you really want to say and stop hiding behind sarcasm. It's dangerous, hurtful, and not nice. And here's a pro tip: Do not let any family member contribute to sarcasm about your partner. Figure out why you feel you can't say what you really want to say.

COMMANDMENT #9

- **Legacy: Leave the Bitch out of your O"bitch"uary**

Imagine your days are up and everyone is at your funeral. What would you like them to remember about you? What kind of person were you and how did you live your life? As a teacher, I remember my guiding metaphor was, "children won't remember what you taught them, but they will remember how you treated them and how they felt around you." This is also true of our relationships. In the grand scheme of things, what legacy would you like to leave behind?

COMMANDMENT #10

- **Stop Keeping a List and Stop Name Calling**

Get rid of that imaginary list you have on your partner. You know, the time you two fought in the restaurant and never talked about it? Either start fresh, or talk about it once you have done some of the work involved to move you away from your unhealthy patterns. While we are on the topic of fighting, stop calling each other names! Don't do it. It hurts, it stings, it's childish. Grow up and be respectful even when you don't like each other.

Ok, so here's the deal: You owe it to your relationship to consider the ideas you've amassed in reading this book! You've tried self help books, different therapists, marriage retreats, but none of it worked. But if we do this together, with your will power, we can make something magical happen. No, I'm not a miracle worker. But I've got important news for you: You are! You can do this, and I want to help you. That is my purpose in writing this book. I.WANT.TO.HELP! It is my passion and my purpose in life to help others. Are you sceptical? Have you thrown in the towel? Are you just trying to get to the end of this book because you've come this far? At the very worst, you spent a few dollars on this book that you could have allocated to something else. But my hope is that you will be inspired by the tools I've collected from the many sources and experiences I've had in working with couples. I've also opened up, showing you my innermost fears, my challenges, and also my triumphs. Well, our triumphs—mine and Paul's. I've purposely done this because I think there's a lot to be learned from everyone's challenges. We all win and we all suffer. Though my story is unique, it's also universal in the sense that Paul and I are a work in progress. Who isn't, right? As I mentioned in the prologue, Paul and I have had our fair share of trials and tribulations. We've gone through years of health scares, money trouble, and years in which we didn't know how we were going to stay a couple. But we've done it and continue to do it. And do you know what? We used the very tools I've provided in this book. This means that you can do it too. You have the power to make it happen—to be a miracle worker. It's truly possible.

Key takeaways:

1. The gray area is a great place to be, instead of black and white, all or nothing thinking.
2. Use the 10 tips above, they work!

CHAPTER 9

Secure Attachment

"Marriage is grand, but divorce is fifty grand. It's cheaper to stay married!"

—DAVE RAMSEY—

My dog has an awareness of when it should be feeding time. 8 am and 6 pm are generally the times we feed our fur baby. If we get busy, we can rely on Lola, our Husky Shepherd baby, to tell us to get our butts in gear and fill her slow-eater dish. Within 5.7 seconds, she'll eat a cup and a half of kibble, regardless of any constraint we put in place. I'm not so sure I'd call Lola fully aware and actualized, especially when it comes to food. But Lola counts on us to feed her. She spent the first six months of her life in a very remote northern community, where she didn't belong to anyone per se, but acted more like a restless vulture. She'd circle homes in that remote community, surviving on scraps and the neighbourhood's kindness, whenever there was leftover food to be shared. Lola has since grown to adapt to life as a trained house pet. She's nine years old and loves eating food more than any other pastime. Unfortunately, she'll even sneak a piece of paper towel if there's a drop of bacon juice on it!

When Lola sees the savoury food in her dish, she goes into a mode that, at one time, was very scary for us as her family. At first, it was pretty aggressive. But over the years, with a lot of training, she's become far less aggressive during feeding time. Nevertheless, during feeding time, she's so hyper focused that not even the Dog Whisperer himself could get her to "leave it." Pavlov's response may be at play here; but make no mistake, Lola's 5.7 second eating ability is a natural instinct based on her previous experiences.. Either way, survival mode can kick in very quickly, as an instinct that can serve as both a need *and* a habit. Lola was able to protect herself as a puppy by using her survival instinct, which kicked in automatically. Nine years later, that instinct is still triggered at feeding time and whenever she's around food. But the speed of her eating, not even chewing one piece of kibble, has become detrimental to her health, not to mention her teeth. Oh, and Lola can clear the room with one silent but deadly "pfffff...".

What about you? How have you protected yourself when your needs aren't being met? Is it possible that your protection method is detrimental to your relationship? Are you approachable during these times of distress or can you clear the room just like Lola's bad smelly ones, with your behaviour? Perhaps you become clingy, bitchy, become a jerk, give the silent treatment, or employ another survival method in order to protect yourself from harm. In Lola's case, the harm would have been starvation. Think about a time when you've felt unloved, refused, and as a result, not at your best. How did you show up, both literally and figuratively? In chapter two, we learned about attachment styles and how we are often a product of what we were taught and how we interpret our experiences as children. I will go one step further and say that some theorists believe we seek our unmet needs in the partners we choose. Well, perhaps it's no wonder your partner is so much like your mother or father. It makes perfect sense, doesn't it? But unfortunately, we will still be left with the void. Whether your mother was like Mother Teresa or Kim Kardashian, even well-intended experiences can have a negative impact on our attachment style. Yes, even Mother Teresa probably *s**t the bed!* As a result, we often create protection methods, and enter into a cycle with a loved one, that will often exacerbate the *exact negative self interpretation* we are trying to avoid through protection. This is a significant concept, so allow me to explain.

Ugh. Are you saying that my habits are dog-like, Jennifer? Well, somewhat; yes. Your habits are kind of dog-like. Remember when we learned about fear and what happens to us when our safety becomes threatened? When someone is in a state of fear, we often lose the ability to think rationally, resorting instead to a primitive way of thinking. In psychological terms, we're reverting to the reptilian brain. That is, the part that kicks in when we need to survive and focus on self preservation. Any danger, physical, emotional...etc...can be the catalyst for our brain to switch to the reptilian brain. When our bodies sense emotional danger which could include the inability to connect to your partner, an atmosphere of mistrust and fear can be created. Or it could refer to the inability to fill a void that relates to past trauma. These are just two examples but there are many more types of emotional danger. As a result, your body tells you to protect yourself since it feels like it's in danger. But you've got something a dog doesn't have: you've got the ability to become intensely self-aware and use your imagination to create new outcomes based on your desires. You have the ability to heal using various means, including therapy, self care, or surrounding yourself with people who encourage you in a nurturing way. Just as Lola will eat cardboard without thinking, so too will we resort back to our old habits when we regress into survival mode. But if you become more aware of things like your *protection methods*, then there is tremendous hope on the horizon for you.

How we act automatically while in survival mode may always be part of our behaviour, but instead of allowing it to take over 10 out of 10 times during a conflict, would you be able to get to a point where it happens only 8 out of 10 times? This would mean that you would need to be aware of when it happens, so you can choose to thrive instead of gravitating to your innate need to "survive." *What does this look like? What are you talking about Jennifer?*

Well, first off, check out this Quick Tip :

Quick Tip:

Scale:

1 ------------------------5------------------------ 10

Where are you on this scale? Imagine this scale when you read the scenario below. How could you stay regulated and out of survival protective mode (10/10) or a total shut down (1/10). How can you stay in the middle, a.k.a. in the grey? Remember that all or nothing thinking from earlier chapters, and how detrimental it can be to our lives? Gray is a great place to hang out.

Scenario:

Your partner comes home, and you are exhausted, tired, and annoyed about the dishes they left on the table last night. Do you:

a) You get annoyed, call them a "douchebag" in a funny manner, and tell them they need to clean up their own mess? After all, they made the mess.

b) Ignore it, but feel really annoyed. For the next week, you feel resentment and remain silent when you are in the same room?

c) Tell them you're struggling with exhaustion, and would be so grateful if they could take the reins for the evening by cleaning up the dishes that aren't clean.

Which would you choose and why?

_____

_____

_____

_____

_____

_____

_____

In my opinion, option a and b would be a "survival mode" choice. By choosing a or b, it may well feel easier in the moment, because you've become conditioned to that response– it's become your default choice. Default is easier than having to make a choice and enter the unknown, right? But option c would be in line with moving towards a badass relationship, a.k.a., a secure attachment with your partner.

If we break it down:

Option (a) (8 or 9/10) would be a parental, aggressive, controlling answer that we have all given and to which we can easily default. Yes, your partner may have been a douche-bag in the moment, but bringing it to their attention will not keep the emotional connection open. Name calling is hurtful and detrimental to one another and should be taken off the table, completely.

Option b (8 or 9/10) is a passive aggressive way to avoid the conflict but to increase the tension within the home. Not only will you and your relationship suffer, but your family will too. Children can sense when something is wrong. (More on this in my next book.) It's ok if your children know you aren't feeling your best. It takes the guessing out of it and keeps them in a safe state. Not knowing but feeling something is out of sync is a very scary place for children (and adults).

Option c (4-8/10) is an example of how you could share where you're at emotionally, and what you need in the moment. This honest response will both honour yourself, your partner, and most importantly, be a respectful option for honouring your relationship. That third entity is so important and needs to be protected.

You may not be at the place where you can choose option c just yet. And that's okay. You may currently be in an overprotective state and have escalated conflicts that require professional support. If this is the case, I would recommend an Emotionally Focused Therapy (EFT) Therapist who has experience and formal training in this type of counselling. Option C takes work, and an openness from both ends. Option C is an example of what a secure attachment response would look like. Interestingly, even when you become securely attached to your partner, you will still have conflict! That's okay too!! (Feel free to breathe a deep breath of relief—conflict is natural.) When I have a couple come to me and say, "We never fight actually, no conflicts really, we just grew apart," is when I call *bulls**t*. Not only is conflict a part of relationships, it's a necessary element to becoming emotionally connected again. If neither person is showing up to the conflict, (and I don't mean two people avoiding each other with tension) then it may be too late to get them reconnected. Not showing up may indicate that the damage may have gone on too long and both partners have either lost interest or given up on the relationship.

A secure attachment style will determine how you handle conflict and how adept you and your partner are at maintaining an emotional connection—especially in the midst of conflict. As you contemplate and bring awareness to your attachment style, ask yourself if you're able to verbalize what you need in the moment (like in the above scenario) or whether you need some space to process and define the nature of the conflict. Can you give your partner the benefit of the doubt, believe in them, forgive them, and work towards being committed to them and this process? If you can, this is the key to a secure attachment. Emotional connection will allow you to thrive, maintain clarity, give space to share feelings, and provide a feeling of fulfillment. If you've been filling the void with other means, there's a great chance that when you work on a secure attachment, your protective mechanisms (your void-fillers) will begin to erode. No more drugs, alcohol, compulsive shopping, gambling, porn... These fillers are some of the ways to fulfill a void, as mentioned in the early chapters. So, are you ready to fill your void with love, with understanding, and grace? It will feel so good. Come with me and try it!

This book has given you ample guidance to start you on a path towards a more emotionally secure bond with your partner. With this will come a sense of peace and respect amongst the two of you. Imagine a life in which you feel emotionally safe to share, and know you will be comforted. You will be validated and heard at the hardest of times. You will be able to easily connect to your partner and have a positive view of both yourself, your partner, and your relationship. You will enjoy being alone, and will love being together. You will be flexible, adaptable, and will come from a place of unconditional love. That means, you will not put conditions on your love. You will not withhold love or ignore each other, but will be a grown up with big girl or boy pants pulled all the way up. Your unconditional love will be an ongoing venture together. You will honour your relationship, the third entity, ahead of each other; which is, of course, the relationship! What a sweet deal.

THE STORY OF...
...crickets...crickets...

Yes, the anecdote is blank. No, it's not because I used a cheap publisher. It's empty because I don't have an example of anyone with an iron-clad secure attachment style. I have yet to meet anyone with a 100% secure attachment. The research may show differently, but from my experience and hours upon hours of working with different couples, people, and being in a helper role for the last twenty-five years, I have come to realize that every single one of us have scars that have deeply impacted us and have left an imprint on our attachment styles. These imprints, or injuries, have shaped us and have had a profound effect on how we operate. We make sense of the world around us and the people we meet from the lens of a scarred person. Some of us have more scars than others, which is shitty and unfair. I wouldn't be able to explain the depth of just how sad some stories are that I have heard in my office. However, I have also heard stories full of resilience, grace, adaptability, and love. Many people have overcome their painful experiences and have picked themselves up to forge a path towards a secure attachment. Now, I am not trying to be a downer. I'm merely being honest to a fault in order to advise you that you are the norm. *We* are the norm. We all have lived experiences from which we can learn or suffer. It's our choice. We can become adaptable or become maladaptive. Again, it's our choice. We can have love in our hearts or hate in our hearts. Our choice. We can acknowledge when we hurt others or we can fight it and/or avoid it. You guessed it: our choice. So, what's your choice? How do you want to live the next 1,500 weeks? That's right, if you are 50, you have the equivalent of 1,500 weeks left to live. If you are 40, you have the equivalent of 2,000 weeks. So it's your choice how you want those weeks to be.

My Bold & Brave Diary...

What choice will you make? Are you ready to commit to this? Where are you at this moment?

_____

_____

_____

_____

_____

_____

_____

_____

_____

_____

_____

_____

_____

_____

_____

If you chose to stay where you are, maybe you can pass this book onto someone else or make it into a piece of decor (think book ends, paper weights, coasters, mosquito smackers). If you choose to move forward in the direction of a secure attachment and get the relationship you have always wanted, here are the steps to get there.

Step 1: Become aware of where you are presently, in your relationship. good/bad/complicated/so-so...

Step 2: Set a small goal that's attainable in the next week. For example, pick one thing that's a nuisance to you and try to face it. Talk to your partner about making changes, and complete most of the daredevil diaries in this book.

Step 3: Every day, look in the mirror and say, "I can do this, and I deserve this. My partner can do this, and they deserve this. We can do this for our relationship (and our family)."

Step 4: Apply the knowledge, tips, and explicit details from this book immediately. Do the best you can. Refer to this guide often and remember you are human; it will take time.

Step 5: Find a kickass therapist who knows their stuff, is understanding, and does not give you advice or try to solve your problems (instead they write a book to get all the advice out that they can't say in session).

Step 6: Practice kindness towards yourself, and your partner. Find love in your heart and remember why you chose your partner in the first place. If you've both decided to part ways after this experience, do it with kindness and grace. Take the "bitch" out of your "o-bitch-uary" so that you can have a loving, kind legacy after your 1,500 weeks are up. Make that epitaph a beauty!

Is love enough to stay together? Hell to the NO! Love is enough to bring you together, but you will need much more to make it last as I just hammered home over the last eight chapters. Whether you are struggling with your self esteem, childhood traumas, relationship roles, money, sex, coparenting, or are just bored with your relationship, think about how great it would feel to wake up knowing how to work these things out with your loved one. Even if it isn't with the same partner you are with now, the work still needs to be done. The problem isn't your current partner, and the solution isn't to break up either. The key to a secure, loving relationship is to work on all the things that are a part of your baggage, or are an obstacle in front of you. Once you deal with this, you will have a clear vision of what you want in a relationship, which can include your current partner or future one: your choice. Think of this like pushing out a baby (or a kidney stone). You must labour to get to the end. Moments of difficulty will ebb and flow, like contractions every 4-5 minutes. You must breathe!! Then the head will crown, and oh boy (or other), you will want to quit. I remember that moment well. I was willing to walk around with a head sticking out of me, because I didn't have an ounce of energy left. I asked the doc to just leave it be, I would adjust. But, somehow, I was able to continue. It's imperative for our wellbeing that we muster up that energy, make one final push, and *voila*, a beautiful bouncing baby. The labour and pain is always worth it in the end. In fact, most of the time, all that pain and those memories will fade as your level of fulfillment increases, filling the void with love, compassion and understanding. And, you will be so proud that you were able to see it through. Either way, you have a choice to direct your energy towards a secure relationship with intention or revert to old survival habits. Indeed, if you have the courage and the fortitude, the feeling of attaining a secure attachment is euphoric. Can you imagine what it would be like to love without hurt in the way? To love without resentment in the way? Does your partner feel like the fruit to your loom, the milk to your shake, the ice to your cream? You know you belong together but can't stand to be together? Or perhaps you have children together and want them to grow up with both parents present. Either way, before thinking of breaking up or leaving, become secure in your relationships, become secure in yourself, and then make the decision. Insecure attachment behaviours will follow you wherever you go, until you heal and then change them. Do this with your present partner, then decide. Once you become aware of what secure attachment looks and feels like, you might just attract a different type of person than before. Remember, your unmet needs will no longer drive your behaviour, you will understand them, and will learn how to manage yourself and ask for what you need. You deserve this love, and it's completely within reach.

THE BOTTOM LINE UNFILTERED...

We are never done growing. Does that sound exhausting or exciting? For me, it depends on the day. We all have good and bad days, and growth feels much harder on the bad ones. On those days, I sometimes catch myself comparing my messy reality to the flawless images we see on TV—like the perfect woman in the insurance commercials with her green smoothie and pristine kitchen. In those moments, my frustration gets the best of me. But then I remind myself: I'm human. I have my faults, doubts, and self-sabotaging behaviours. On good days, I feel invincible and wouldn't dream of being so negative.

I'm this transparent because, as a therapist, I believe honesty is essential for helping others. This final chapter won't sugarcoat things. It's a straightforward look at how hard it can be to show ourselves grace and self-love, especially when we make mistakes. Our moods often shift based on our self-perception, and that affects our relationships.

Have you noticed the baggage you're carrying? It's heavy, isn't it? But there are many ways to lighten that load—ways that don't have to be scary or lonely, and ways that you can tackle at your own pace. It's so easy to blame others for what we feel is happening to us. I can get jealous of my husband's ability to compartmentalize and wish I could switch off my brain.

My worries often keep me up at night while my husband sleeps soundly. I sometimes wonder how he can rest so easily when my mind races through thoughts about everything from our son's class trip to the dog's mood and looming bills. My thoughts can feel like a tangled mess of spaghetti, while men seem to think more like waffles: one thought at a time, neatly compartmentalized. Although it's easy to feel resentful when I'm on the brink of a meltdown, I've learned that my husband is simply in his "sleep square." He might not fully understand my thought process, but he is always ready to offer love and support when I need it. Over time, I've learned to communicate my needs: just love and some space. We are all works in progress, and embracing that journey helps us grow together.

Now it's your turn. Will you embrace your own journey and commit to the work it requires? Whether you're just starting or already on your way, remember this: you are absolutely worth it! You have the strength and resilience to succeed—you're a total badass! Believe in yourself, because I certainly do. I'll be cheering you on every step of the way. You've got this!

Key takeaways:

1. Humans often develop protective modes from past hurts that can strain relationships, but it's our responsibility to change them so we can be more secure in our attachment.

2. A secure attachment takes work, and dedication. There may still be conflict but you will know how to deal with it as a team.

3. We have a choice in how we proceed in our relationships.

Epilogue

Thank you for taking the time to read my book. It took me a few years to complete, and after much trial and error, I finally got there. My goal was always to show that I, too, have to work for a badass relationship every single day. We make choices in every moment, through challenges and experiences with our loved ones. I mess up, just like you. I make mistakes, just like you. I never wanted this book to feel like I was some distant psychotherapist judging you from behind glasses while you lie on a couch. Instead, I hoped you'd imagine us having a casual coffee, talking about what might work and what might not. Everything in this book—tips, examples, insights—comes from my 25 years of experience, and I offer it to you with the hope that it helps. I'm right here with you, cheering you on.

As for my husband, Paul, we're still happily married—most of the time! We work hard at it, and while some days are easy, others are not. But the good days definitely outnumber the bad. Along the way, we made big decisions, like moving across the country to carve out a life that's truly ours, free from distractions and focused on what matters to us.

Paul's health remains a challenge, and he had a second major surgery in 2017. While he will always have physical limitations, he has grown into an even more incredible man because of them. He's become more loving and caring than ever, much like my father. I consider myself one lucky woman.

Appendix

Common Characteristics of Attachment Styles
Note: This is not a diagnostic assessment, but a guide to help identify which attachment style to explore further.

ATTACHMENT TYPE	Anxious:	Avoidant:	Disorganized:
	• I am often preoccupied, overbooked, not attuned or present in the conversation. • I often belittle myself openly and will lift others up in excess. • I need constant reassurance from my partner. • Emotions are scary and intense.	• I may seem uninterested in anything remotely serious or may crack many jokes to avoid being uncomfortable. • I often will change the subject if faced with conversations about emotions. • I may belittle or dismiss others to avoid all emotional engagement. • Emotions are uncomfortable and gross.	• I may seem avoidant at times or may dismiss others. • I may belittle others and their emotions. but could also seem genuinely interested. • If I was interested, it would stop there. I would not be attuned to others. • Emotions are scary and uncomfortable
WHY	• I had an unavailable, preoccupied parent/caregiver.	• I had a strict, emotionally absent parent/caregiver.	• I had a traumatic childhood and/or an abusive parent. • My parent/caregiver was scary and unpredictable.

CHARACTERIS-TICS	• I have a neg-ative view of myself but a positive view of others. • I have an intense fear of rejection and aban-donment. • I can be "clingy" in relationships. • I often feel unworthy of love.	• I have a positive view of myself and often a negative view of others. • I tend to reject others before they can reject themselves • I am often closed off	• I have a neg-ative view of myself and a negative view of others. • I can include both anxious and avoidant characteristics. • I am often unpredictable with my emo-tions.
BEHAVIOUR (protection from un-comfortable feelings)	• I will pursue arguments or conflicts to prove my point or get my way. • I seek vali-dation from my partner often. • I will con-tinually ask for help if I need it and won't stop until I get what I think I need which is to be validated/recognized. • I often overshare personal information to others.	• I will shut down when faced with conflict, often will default to the flight response. • I will avoid be-ing vulnerable and intimate. • I will seem independent and self-reliant. I've been known as a "loner" who beats to my own drum. • I will downplay emotions, and dismiss others. • I won't ask for help since it is a weakness.	• I'll have a difficult time trusting any-one. • I know I need my partner but I often want them to go away, but then want them back, then to go away…etc… • It feels scary to get close to anyone.

Emotions

HAPPINESS
- Joy
- Delight
- Contentment
- Satisfaction
- Bliss
- Cheerfulness
- Elation

LOVE
- Affection
- Adoration
- Devotion
- Fondness
- Warmth
- Caring
- Attachment

CONFIDENCE
- Assurance
- Certainty
- Boldness
- Self-assurance
- Self-reliance
- Courage
- Conviction

SADNESS
- Sorrow
- Grief
- Melancholy
- Despair
- Heartache
- Mourning

DISGUST
- Revulsion
- Contempt
- Loathing
- Distaste
- Aversion
- Repulsion

JEALOUSY
- Envy
- Covetousness
- Resentfulness
- Bitterness
- Spite
- Grudge
- Rivalry

ANGER
- Rage
- Fury
- Annoyance
- Resentment
- Irritation
- Outrage

SURPRISE
- Amazement
- Astonishment
- Shock
- Wonder
- Bewilderment
- Disbelief

FEAR
- Anxiety
- Worry
- Dread
- Terror
- Panic
- Apprehension

GUILT
- Remorse
- Regret
- Shame
- Contrition
- Embarrassment
- Apology